✔ KU-826-738

Organization and Democracy Series • 2

WITHDRAWN

ORGANIZING AROUND ENTHUSIASMS

Patterns of Mutual Aid in Leisure

By Paul Hoggett and Jeff Bishop

THE LIBRARY
NEWMAN COLLEGE
BARTLEY GREEN
BIRMINGHAM B32 3NT

Class No. 306.48
Barcode. N 0080739 7
Author. .... BIS

Comedia Publishing Group
9 Poland Street, London W1V 3DG

N 0080739 7

This new series is concerned with questions of management as they apply to campaigning and voluntary organizations and also to the various movements of social change. Some books will attempt to define the existing range of self managed activity, while others will discuss and publicise ways of working that are both effective and congruent with democratic aspirations and principles.

Too often democracy and self management have meant inertia and inaction. While the series opposes the blind extension of management ideas into organizations with social goals it considers that worthy incompetence needs to be overcome. Series editor Patrick Wright is currently head of the Management Development Unit at the National Council for Voluntary Organisations.

First published in 1986 by Comedia Publishing Group
9 Poland Street, London W1V 3DG.

ISBN 0.906890.85.3

British Library Cataloguing in Publication Data
Bishop, Jeff
    Organizing around enthusiasms: patterns of mutual aid
    in leisure
    1. Leisure—Social aspects—Great Britain
    I. Title
    306'.48'0941 GV75

Cover Design by Andrzej Krauze

Typeset by Photosetting, 6 Foundry House, Yeovil, Somerset BA20 1NL.

Printed in Great Britain by Unwin Brothers Ltd.,
The Gresham Press, Old Woking, Surrey.

Trade Distribution by George Philip Ltd.

Acknowledgements

There is little doubt about the first acknowledgement – that must be to the hundreds of people to whom we spoke during our research. On the majority of occasions that we have been able to explain to them our conclusions, the response has been positive. Some have, however, reacted strongly to our analysis, to our over-complication of what to them is 'just running a group'. We share some of their anxieties, but hope that our broader perspective will enable people to see the pitfalls ahead. In general, we hope our description and analysis conveys their world successfully and thank them for their remarkable openness and help.

Our second acknowledgement is to our research sponsors, the Social Science Research Council (now the Economic and Social Research Council) and the Sports Council. Their joint Steering Committee retained trust in us even through the latter part of our initial year when we were diverted considerably off the preordained path. Their enthusiastic help and support was indispensable to the project.

Finally, we would like to express our thanks to Pam Aldren for transforming our amateur typing and scribbling into a professional and presentable text for the publisher.

THIS BOOK IS DEDICATED TO WILLIAM MORRIS

'Yet I think that to all living things there is a pleasure in the exercise of their energies. But a man at work, making something which he feels will exist because he is working at it and wills it, is exercising the energies of his mind and soul as well as of his body. Memory and imagination help him as he works and, as part of the human race, he creates. If we work thus we shall be men, and our days will be happy and eventful. Thus worthy work carries with it the hope of pleasure in rest, the hope of the pleasure in our using what it makes and the hope of pleasure in our daily creative skill.'

Useful Work Versus Useless Toil

Contents

1. Introduction   1

2. Group cameos: some sketches   9

3. Mutual aid in leisure   29

4. Leisure sub-cultures   43

5. The contribution of individuals to groups   59

6. The environment of groups   72

7. The structure and dynamic of communal leisure
    organizations   98

8. Conclusions   121

    References   131

Chapter 1

Introduction

Much of this introduction was written at home during the evening yet, despite the considerable enjoyment the authors received from writing this book, the activity could hardly be called leisure. At the same time as our 'amateur' hands were striking the typewriter keys, hundreds of thousands of people around the country were indulging in 'leisure' activity, putting in at least as much hard 'work' as we are doing and probably much of it in a far more 'professional' and no doubt skilled manner. It is partly because of such contradictions that leisure remains such an elusive and diverse territory – we all know of people who put far more effort and care into their leisure activities than into 'paid work'!

The concern of this book is with activity which is freely given yet typically assumes the form of highly skilled and imaginative work, whilst remaining leisure and not employment. We wish to look at the self-confessed amateurs who go about their activity in a highly professional manner and yet for whom the 'social aspects' of their pursuit are indispensable. Our focus, therefore, is the world of the enthusiast, particularly those who indulge their passions collectively by participating in groups. Our own research suggests that such activity far exceeds all other forms of self-organized activity, whether in housing, health, or whatever.

In this study we will use the phrase 'communal leisure group' (or simply 'group') as a general label to refer to the clubs, societies, associations, etc., within which such activities take place. We use the term 'group' rather than 'organization' because of its connotations of intimacy and familiarity. Although a club may actually be quite large, its participants will nevertheless refer to it in terms of 'the group' whereas they would not dream of referring to their factory or office in the same way. We use the term 'communal' because of its connotations of community, even though in many instances it is more appropriate to speak of a 'community of interest' binding enthusiasts together, rather than a neighbourhood identity. The word 'communal' also suggests 'commune', the tradition of self-organization which has struggled to remain alive within industrial capitalism. Regarding 'leisure', we are aware of, and concerned about, its slightly demeaning connotations as something not really to be taken very seriously. However, whilst our enthusiasts are engaged in leisure, this activity is also an essential, perhaps *the* essential, component of our national, regional and local culture.

If we were to attempt to calculate the economic value of the immense amount of time, materials, resources and simple cash which goes into communal leisure, the figures would be astonishing. Yet the very suggestion is in a way an insult to the thousands who contribute their time – either as members or organizers of clubs – in making such a diverse range of leisure activities possible. It is precisely this freedom from economic measures, and from the trappings of the commercialized world of leisure, that attracts people into such groups and enables them to consider what might seem to be work (twenty hours a week perhaps for a club secretary) as leisure. However, leisure is fast becoming a new focus of interest for many sections of society. Private business is no longer simply responding to market demand; it is beginning to create demand. Local government is beginning to co-ordinate its various leisure activities – almost every week there are advertisements for the post of 'Director of Leisure' in newly created departments. A new leisure 'profession' is emerging, as an amalgamation of three formerly separate institutes, and its members are beginning to demand graduate entry and professional control. There is, inevitably, a growing area of academic debate, as well as a fairly new academic journal, *Leisure Studies*.

Surprisingly, despite such developments, remarkably little is known about a major and precious element in the bedrock of our national culture; namely the activities of the many thousands of small groups engaged communally in sports, arts, crafts and hobbies. The research on which this book is based was therefore a journey of discovery. But such a statement demands instant qualification. In Adelaide (Australia), there is a mural with the slogan 'Aborigines Discovered Captain Cook'. To suggest (as school history still does) that the opposite was true is really no more than cultural imperialism and is a stance we feel we should resist in our own documentation of this recently 'discovered' leisure territory. Not surprisingly, many aborigines would have preferred Cook (and all those who followed) to have sailed on by, and we too must be alert to the fact that we might shine too strong and analytical a light on the groups we studied, expose the ambiguities and contradictions of their lives and thus damage them. This caution has therefore affected our whole approach both to the research and to this book. We try, in the chapters which follow, to analyse and describe but also to celebrate; to attempt to convey to the reader some of the excitement, enjoyment and commitment shared by almost all of those to whom we spoke. However, we feel strongly that it is only by understanding and appreciating the nature of the many very different groups that their invaluable contribution to our national cultural lives can be protected and then enhanced.

It should be emphasized from the beginning that 'groups' are in no way merely the setting in which particular activities take place – they are not just a means to an end. If that were true such groups would be of no more significance than sports halls or community centre buildings. In fact, groups offer valuable social and organizational experiences in their own right. A local ornithology society is an entity in its local community; moreover, it is part of a regional, national (and international) natural history network, its members are probably also members of the Royal Society for the Protection of Birds and it may be part of a very active and diverse, public sector supported community centre. Yet *that* ornithology society is very different from another one just three miles down the road. One is friendly, open and sociable, the other very serious and 'professional'. The two are very different in character, fulfilling very different social needs. Moreover, it becomes clear from almost everybody we interviewed that a group is both 'different from' and 'more than' the sum of its members, with an 'existence' which can continue even after all original members have left.

Such statements run counter to what we would regard as a continuing thrust within leisure policy and research which we can term 'functionalism'. From this perspective, which has its roots in the 'Sports Planning' area of leisure,[1] people are alleged to have leisure needs (and can therefore also suffer from 'leisure lack'). Thus, if it can be determined that in a particular area there are X people wishing to play squash, Y to play badminton and Z to play tennis, then one-to-one private or public provision should follow. Any wider social or cultural aspects of the activity are ignored or subordinated to the functional aspect of the chosen pursuit. We might suggest, conversely, that a wish to play squash or tennis *follows from* a wish to establish oneself in a particular social, cultural and organizational setting; that the activity is almost a 'front' or 'excuse'.

Why do people invest their groups with meanings and identities which grant them such an important social role? We believe that involvement in such groups offers people something probably unique in our society: the chance to come together with others to create or participate for collective benefit and enjoyment rather than for sale to an anonymous audience or purchaser. This is why their continued existence is important and why these groups are so keen to assert their independence. At the same time, it is easy to see how this fragile independence might be eroded, for example, by commercialization of leisure.

In order to provide the reader with a more concrete understanding of the dynamics of communal leisure groups, in the following chapter we present a series of sketches or 'cameos' of individual groups. These 'sketches', deliberately chosen to illustrate the diversity of such groups, provide a picture of these organizations' routines, crises and ways of handling things as seen by the enthusiasts themselves. The cameos also discuss current dilemmas or problems for some of the groups. We do not feel the groups we sketch are necessarily typical, but they do offer a flavour or feeling for the world of the enthusiast.

Chapter 3 examines the significant nature of communal leisure groups as organized forms of mutual aid through which enthusiasts combine together to produce goods and services for their own enjoyment, while Chapters 4, 5 and 6 cover the context within which groups operate. Chapter 4 posits the existence of a large number of *sub-cultures* within which activities take place. Thus a folk dancing sub-culture, for example, will have a specialized language, a circuit of events, a history, attitudes towards improvisation, etc., which each group will either accept or mould quietly to its own members and circumstances. Chapter 5 considers *individual enthusiasts* and the needs and values which lead them to join a group, then find a role within it. Chapter 6 discusses the *environment* within which a group operates. This includes the local community, leagues and associations (a formal and institutional part of sub-cultures), the commercial sector, the public sector and the independent sector. Chapter 7 looks at ways in which groups handle this extraordinary diversity. It illustrates the various methods they employ, sometimes unconsciously, to use positively and build from diversity, rather than reduce it. We also consider some of the problems which occur when groups fail to raise some aspects of their working to a more conscious level.

In the final chapter we consider some of the wider implications of our research. No solutions are offered, merely a suggestion that the world of enthusiasts and their forms of self-organization in groups and sub-cultures is of major significance and must be understood *in its own terms* if it is not to become another extinct phenomenon.

The research project

In the late 1970s the (then) Social Science Research Council became interested in the emergent area of leisure research and was (as it were) met from the other direction by some from the practical leisure world seeking a more rigorous grounding for some of their continuing debates. This led to the formation of a Joint Panel of the SSRC and Sports Council which, after commissioning some outline studies of the territory[2] proceeded to commission several major projects.[3] One topic outlined for further work[4] was what has come to be described as the voluntary sector in leisure. It was recognized that little was known about the number, membership, structure, problems and potential of the thousands of groups in Great Britain, nor about their relationship to private and public leisure provision.

The outcome of this discussion was a project entitled 'The Operation of the Voluntary Sector in Leisure'. The School for Advanced Urban Studies competed successfully for the contract. At this stage Paul Hoggett became involved and, once the project was decided upon, Jeff Bishop joined him. Initially the contract was for one year, commencing early in 1982, but with a degree of commitment to two further stages. When time came to review the work, its outcomes were already beginning to appear somewhat different from those anticipated; moreover, the Joint Panel had chosen to spend a greater proportion of its available finance on dissemination. Consequently a second stage only was agreed, to be spread over fifteen months, in order to allow time for contacts to be developed.

In essence, the aim of the project can be expressed very simply: we were aiming to find out 'what makes groups tick'. There were several overlapping elements to the work, although they can be summed up under three broadly sequential stages.

Making contact

Two areas were chosen for study, partly to provide what we hoped would be a contrast. One was Kingswood District (encompassing as it does several areas and pre-1974 urban districts). This is a suburban crescent to the east of Bristol, mostly post-1919 housing coalescing around what were distinct villages in the last century (of which Kingswood itself was and still is one). Politically a very marginal area, it varies from fairly cheap owner-occupied housing to fairly wealthy suburbs such as Downend. To some extent the area depends upon Bristol for some major services, but is nevertheless full of many social networks, partly resulting from the strong, local Methodist tradition.

The second study area was Leicester. It was never intended that our work should cover the whole of the city (although again it was a district council boundary which had most influence), so, after initial contacts, a 'wedge' to the north-east of the city was selected. This incorporated the more recent inner-city council estates of St Matthews, the older owner-occupied housing of Belgrave (now a major Asian community), the run-down white working-class estate of Northfields and the aspirant edge-of-city suburb of Rushey Fields.

After a time a list of groups emerged, often with little more than the address of a contact person. The great surprise came in Kingswood where a list provided by the local authority of eighty groups quickly became 315, at which point we stopped searching! The minimal information available from the lists made it impossible to make any reasonable selection for groups to contact and therefore we chose to send out a very brief questionnaire to a large number of those listed. In fact, the questionnaire also provided some very valuable information in its own right. Much of this will be discussed later; a detailed appraisal of our methods is available in the final research report.[5]

Having studied the questionnaires and produced some workable criteria for selecting groups, we derived a shortlist and started to arrange interviews. The research brief, for reasons which seemed sensible at the time, excluded coverage of political, uniformed and religious groups. Moreover, both the general sampling and the final selection of those to be interviewed focused upon certain types of groups, especially those thought likely to demonstrate independence and organizational variety. In Chapter 3 we list the many types of activities around which groups form and our ideas should be taken in full knowledge of how they might apply differently to very informal fraternities or branches of strong national organizations, such as the National Association of Boys' Clubs.

Interviewing group members

Most of our work involved interviews with members of groups, supported on occasion with visits to events (for example, a natural history talk) or committee meetings. In general, the interviews were with 'officers' – typically a secretary – although there were also some opportunities to meet ordinary members. In fact there were two different types of group study: the 'single interview' and the 'in-depth' study. Typically, an in-depth study would involve interviews with the secretary, chairperson, team captain (or another committee member) and one or two ordinary members, complemented by a visit to an event or meeting.

No formal interview structure was prepared, although most followed a sequence starting with specific questions (history, members, finance, etc.), followed up by deeper probing on key issues (for example, finding new members or coping with the loss of an officer). All interviews were tape-recorded and notes produced later. In the case of in-depth studies, the notes were generally amalgamated into what we have called 'cameos'. The groups selected for interview are listed below, by topic rather than name. Those marked with an asterisk were followed through in depth.

Kingswood	*Leicester*
Saturday League Football Club*	Football Club*
Sunday League Football Club	Football Club*
Hockey Club (Mixed)*	Boxing Club
Adult Disabled Group	Volleyball Club
Metal Detectors' Club	Badminton Club
Youth Band	Square Dance Group
Wives' Group	Handball Club
Cricket Club	Drama Group
Cricket Club*	Aquarists' Society*
Rifle and Pistol Club*	Lapidary Society*
Badminton Club	Swimming Club*
Naturalists' Society*	Morris Dancers*
Boxing Club	Young Disabled Group
Military Modelling Association	Asian People's Association
Ladies' Hockey Club	Boys' Club
Judo Club	Cricket Club*
Weight Training Club	Youth Football Club
Drama Group*	Badminton Set
Cycling Club	Bowling Club
Swimming Club	Gardening Club*
Fishing Club for Disabled	Table Tennis Club
Pensioners' Club	Judo Club
Drama Group	Allotments' Society
Photographic Society*	Badminton Club*
Disabled Persons' Club*	
Bridge Club*	

Contextual studies

While it had always been an intention of the project that it should address questions of public policy, this aspect faded somewhat in the first year, as the assertive independence of groups became clear. Nevertheless the second year of work aimed to examine such issues more formally. Apart from the conventional literature search, the contextual studies were comprised almost entirely of interviews with selected people. There was no set pattern to these and the list evolved over the life of the project. The list included both local authority personnel (such as recreation officers, social workers, planners, youth workers, teachers, community development officers, sports centre and community centre managers, elected councillors) as well as vicars, voluntary workers, Councils of Voluntary Service, Manpower Services Commission teams, officers of leagues, federations and associations, judges, Sports Council officials and commercial sponsors. Again, interviews were recorded and notes written.

Chapter 2

Group cameos: some sketches

It would have been very easy for the authors of this book to assume that each reader knows of the existence of clubs and societies, has possibly experienced them personally and therefore requires no description of the way in which such groups affect their lives. In fact, clubs and societies are so numerous and so widespread that most readers will indeed have had direct or indirect experience. But to assume, therefore, that no restatement of their styles, approaches and activities is necessary would be entirely wrong. Memory is selective and as so much of what happens in groups is regarded as everyday and 'mundane', some description of such groups in detail is essential.

Why, however, are these cameos placed at the beginning of the book rather than at the end, where they might serve to exemplify our analysis? It has been our experience in presenting the evidence from our work in other settings that most people hold in their minds particular preconceptions, perhaps prejudices, about such concepts as 'voluntary sector', 'leisure', 'community' or 'management', which they often apply unconsciously even to their own personal experience of communal leisure groups. Presenting some cameos here, we urge readers to feel free to respond to the pictures offered in terms of such preconceptions. Our hope is that subsequent chapters of the book may then begin to challenge your own peculiar preconceptions and lead to a changed perspective.

Before providing these sketches, we should explain our 'ground rules' about confidentiality. In the introduction we mentioned our two study areas by name, but then referred to our study groups by activity only. From here on in the book all individual groups described in detail will be given false names, as will any members within them whose names might have to be provided. Occasionally reference is made to other clubs, to associations, to places or to people; the majority of these (for example, to the Photographic Alliance) are in fact real organizations, as no confidentiality is necessary.

Five cameos are presented. They are not particularly typical or average. All are based directly upon the spontaneous and unverified comments of those to whom we spoke and they all represent 'snapshots' of groups at the time at which we interviewed members.

Monktonians United Football Club

On a cold winter's night, in the depths of a secondary school campus in east Bristol, the Monktonians United Football club finish their training session with a seven-a-side match on the starkly lit court. Perhaps the commitment and eagerness of the players reflects the chill of the night or perhaps it is seen as a merciful release after the vigorous but little liked skill and fitness training. As the game proceeds, the manager is considering the team selection for the following Saturday, occasionally consulting the trainer or secretary. Nevertheless, it is the manager's choice alone which determines the team, even though he may have no say at all in the details of training.

The Monktonians, or Monks, are now in the top division of the Somerset Senior League, where they have been for a few years after starting originally as an under-elevens team and slowly working their way up through the age groups. This is not typical of local clubs; more commonly they start as one or two discontented players break off from their own club to initiate another. The roots of this unusual beginning lie with the Martin family. The early driving forces of the club were Mick Martin and then his son Steve. The latter started as a player before becoming the second manager (the first during their time as a senior club). Although Mr Martin senior left the club before they found their current ground at Longwood Green Community Centre, he had a role in gaining access to the centre and its pitch, as well as providing (through his contacts as a builder) a lot of help in building the changing rooms. These changing rooms are now of major importance to the future of the club because they are evidently inadequate, proving a major block to the club's future promotion in the league. At the time of our research, the community centre had just received a grant to rebuild the changing rooms and add some further accommodation, offering a chance for the Monks to move up. This is an important change, because at the time they first joined Longwood Green 'there was nothing in it for the centre'. The Monks certainly feel that they have made a major contribution, not just through their first rough building but also because they certainly put more money over the bar than any other club.

There is therefore a symbiotic relationship between the club and the centre. The centre could not manage to acquire the extra facilities without the Monktonians and the Monks could not get a grant simply for themselves to build a pavilion. Who exactly owns, or feels that they own, the new block will be very interesting to see, especially because there have already been some tensions about the pitch. This issue is further complicated because the pitch is rented from the local authority and used by two other teams, including a youth team.

Monks feel that this leads to misuse, to problems when they themselves play on it and ultimately to problems if they seek promotion – as standard of pitch and premises are vetted by the league. (This relationship between club, local centre and public authority will be revealed to be a constant theme of the book.)

Like many clubs in the area, Monks run only one team. However, according to the treasurer, 'it's very difficult with a one-team club. You've got to keep dragging players in because obviously you can get a better player and a bloke can be left out in the cold. You've got to keep him involved. You've still got to keep as large a squad as possible without upsetting people.' Naturally, at what is quite a high standard of play (two or three players worked their way up to semi-pro level before returning to Monks) the wish to play regularly means that there are always players on the move between clubs, although the league has very strict rules about transfers and exchanges of registered players. Monks, as a friendly club, seems to be able to hold its players well, although several youngsters deliberately seek out higher levels if possible before returning to complete their careers with the club. When asked why so many return to the club, some typical answers were: 'They were in a good standard.' 'It doesn't matter what you do on the pitch; as soon as you're back in the bar, everybody's friendly.' 'Monks have got a good name around Bristol.' 'I like it at the club.' It was also clear that the personal effect of the Martins was considerable in encouraging players to come or to stay. The team play their league games at Longwood Green, but are also involved in three local cup competitions which can take them almost anywhere in the area. They have, as yet, had no success in the latter.

Training takes place on a court rented from the local authority on two nights each week. The trainer, an ex-player, said, 'I've always been interested in training. It's probably because I have more experience than anybody in the side. Training had become a bit lax for a while. When you get to this standard, I don't think you expect you've got to be training.'

As at most clubs, attendance at training is mandatory but not everybody comes every time. Most people live in Bristol, although one member now lives in Taunton. In a practice apparently typical at this level of football, there were two players from a club in Frome who join the training because they live much nearer to Bristol.

Apart from the trainer, the manager is a key figure, though his precise role was the subject of some uncertainty amongst players. His role appears to be almost that of an outsider. He can, for example, attend committee meetings but not vote, and he cannot influence training. Essentially he picks the side, attends the matches and gives the half-time pep talk. He also, however, arranges a few tactical sessions on training evenings. The current manager is only the third for the club. He was a player when Steve Martin left, who realised that the club were looking outside for a new manager, did not approve of the names being suggested and offered to take on the role himself, a fact obviously appreciated by the club. He had no experience of managing but considered himself a born leader. He tries to pick up clues from other managers: 'I try to work my way into everyone at a different time. I'm a good listener.'

While the role of team captain might seem quite important, it is and it isn't. According to the current captain, he was chosen by the manager 'because I like shouting on the field. I don't do anything off the field. I just do what the manager decides on. If we don't do well, he'll drop me, captain or not.' Nevertheless, the team captain is automatically on the committee which selects the manager. The last key role is that of secretary, currently occupied by the person who has taken over the inspirational role of the Martins: 'I mean Roger is Monktonians really... he does a tremendous job. Roger is very modest; he doesn't even want a thank-you.'

Roger is one of the committee which includes the secretary, the chairman (a difficult role to fill), the treasurer (recently changed from a friend of the Martins who last played football at school!), the trainer and the captain. As well as being required by their own constitution, such a committee, and many other administrative requirements, are in fact laid down by the league as a precondition of membership. They meet regularly and hold an Annual General Meeting after training – a canny method of making sure they all attend. Many jokes are made about the various roles – according to the treasurer he was chosen because 'I was the only person who could pay the money back if I nicked it. Anyway, the players are not really involved in the committee. They've never thought of that.'

In general, then, the committee is regarded by the players as a necessary evil clearly secondary to the real business of playing football and drinking in the bar after, the main social event of each week to which some wives and girlfriends are also persuaded to come. Although half of them are single, the issue of marriage partners' attitudes emerged during interviews and was seen as a potential imposition on the players' freedom to attend training or stay for a drink (or two) after each game. One younger, recently married member, said: 'She won't mind me playing badminton or squash on a night so long as I play and come home. I can't do that. I've got to have a drink after.'

While this may have an increasing effect on the club if the older players stay rather than move on, the general impression was of a very happy club: 'We go out every week and have a bit of fun. That's what football's there for.' 'We try to take it as seriously as possible.' 'I want to stay. I like it at the club.' 'It's the atmosphere I get playing with Monks ... all the lads are really friendly. Monks is the only club that would stick in my mind as far as the social side is concerned.'

From outside a club such as Monktonians, it is easy to imagine that they are merely one small cog in a complex wheel of hundreds of clubs in several leagues. Yet within the club, despite the regular flow of changes in personnel and the lack of success in cup competitions, a clear sense of identity is evident.

Conwood Naturalists' Society

If you moved to Conwood and were to take a walk along the River Avon, you would come across a signposted nature trail. An encounter with a 'local' might enable you to acquire a copy of the trail guide. A glance at the guide would inform you that the walk was in part devised by the Conwood Naturalists' Society. Perhaps this encounter with an apparently enterprising group would lead you to attend one of the society's meetings, held at the Conwood Folk Centre every month during the winter.

As you arrive you will notice up to twenty-four people, aged on average around forty-five to fifty. Clearly they will all know each other, and some will have arrived in pairs, sharing transport. The chairs will be arranged for a lecture and the slide projector will be set up (both it and the screen are in need of repair). After a very brief introduction the invited speaker starts, using a set of slides to illustrate how the local water authorities are attempting to ensure that their maintenance and improvement work does not damage otter habitats. At the end of a forty-minute talk, only one person, the chairman for the evening, asks a very deferential question. Everybody has clearly enjoyed the session, however, even if no one stays behind for a drink or conversation in the Folk Centre bar. Can this be the same enterprising group which arranged the trail?

To answer this riddle, one must examine the relatively short history of the group and the motivations of some of its early or key members. Their roots lie in the reaction of some local people to a series of natural history talks given at the centre in 1972 by a local teacher who then thought it would be good to start a group. She spoke with a friend and they 'decided to give it a try.' The teacher and some of those who supported the original group are no longer involved. Very quickly, however, they had attracted enough people to make a formal group worthwhile. They arranged a first series of talks, became established, but then, after a few years, numbers dropped, the

Folk Centre raised its charges, and they found cheaper accommodation in a nearby church hall. A little later the church raised its charges, numbers rose again and they moved back to the Folk Centre, this time merely as an outside letting. To many in the Folk Centre the naturalists are still fully involved. The Folk Centre had recently invited them to send a representative to an *ad hoc* committee meeting because, in the warden's words, 'we look on you as part of the Folk Centre'.

This suits the society, because 'we are part of the Folk Centre without being a part of the Folk Centre. It's in everybody's interests to let everything go on quietly without stirring things up,' said the secretary.

In fact several members of the society are also members of other sections at the centre and this was often the way through which they became involved. One woman who came along with a friend was already a centre member. She joined the naturalists, not just because of an interest in birds and walking, but also because her children were growing older and 'probably you could leave them a little more in the evening'. For another member the naturalists appeared on the scene just as he was retiring: 'If you're leading a busy life, particularly one like local government, it eats into your private time. My immediate reaction on retiring was to join a number of societies.' At first his interest in natural history led him to join the large Bristol Naturalists' Society, but 'it was above my head. It was three-quarters university. I was only bathing as it were in the knowledge that was being conveyed to us.' He therefore opted for a more low-key, but also more local, group.

The original intention of the group (partly because of a strong wish to stay small and local) was to be very general, covering flora and fauna and landscape, etc., unlike the Bristol Society which had become specialized and divided into distinct sections. Generalization also raises problems because, as the retired member said: 'people tend to get a bit dissatisfied when they reach the maximum available to them in a general club.' However, as he then continued: 'It's the variety that appeals and makes these groups successful.' His own solution to the lack of specialization is to lecture occasionally himself, for example, on landscape history.

No doubt the difficult balance between generalism and specialism was related to the feeling that many of the members were too passive. The retired member also commented on this by saying that: 'Conwood Naturalists is very amateur. They're dabblers. I suspect a lot of them don't do any original study of their own. A class [note the word] is one-way traffic... you lecture to them but the meat of the meeting should come in the response you get and questions that you are asked. Personally I'm always disappointed when I only get two questions.'

Also there is the question of balance between serious naturalism and the social value of membership of what is clearly a very localized club. One member considered the society to be 'a bit of both. You are out for a good time and you dabble in a variety of activities.' However, there was still the question of whether it should 'be a social club or is it going to be educational?' Clearly many of the ordinary members value the social aspect, yet it appears that those who wish for more can find it by creating it for themselves – hence the lecturing and the trail. The trail was proposed by one or two members. As one said: 'A lot of enthusiasm was displayed but little practical work. By the time it boiled down it was myself plus a retired teacher. The two of us did the survey and later planned the route. I despair of the others doing it.'

The low-key approach is also reflected in the group's management, involving a committee of chairman, vice-chairman, secretary, treasurer and two ordinary members. They are a stable group, 'because it's like any society: you have a core of people who are prepared to work and the rest of the people are prepared to come and go on the fruits of their labour,' as the secretary put it.

Recently a County Wildlife Trust has formed and they are renovating a nearby mill for their headquarters. They also intend to run walks and talks and the Conwood Naturalists are worried about the effect on their own group. 'Whether this means we'll be redundant I couldn't say. I think that personally our society will remain as a quiet backwater where people are interested both in developing their knowledge and the social side of it,' said the secretary. Another member thought that the trust would be too high-powered: 'they'd go once or twice then be back to the Naturalists. The social side is what will bring them back.'

Perhaps there is no easy answer to the apparent contradictions. Perhaps there does not need to be.

Conwood Hockey Club

While we in no sense consciously sought out groups passing through a crisis, it was perhaps inevitable that we would encounter at least one group with serious problems. We certainly came across several coping with birth pangs and one which was so far gone as to be past saving. In the case of the Conwood Hockey Club our first encounter gave no cause for alarm. The secretary willingly told us about their poor performance, but certainly gave no hint of developing problems. When we returned to talk in more depth to people, the problems became apparent, although at that point they appeared soluble. Two years after our first contact, the group was ejected from its pitch and its base in the Folk Centre. We shall watch to see if a phoenix will arise from the ashes.

The root causes of the group's problems may seem almost like three independent issues, although we suspect they are all related – a club having problems about its pitch and with differing views about the value of competitiveness will probably not attract good new players, will therefore decline and descend in a spiral which is difficult to break. The club were in dispute with the cricket club whose pitch they shared. They experienced divergent views about the value of sociability and competitiveness and there was a crisis of confidence in the management and its relationship to on-the-pitch leadership. What finally caused the rift with the Folk Centre we do not know.

So what happened? The club was not terribly old (unlike many hockey clubs with seventy- or eighty-year histories) and it had had a chequered career even before we spoke to its members. It was started in 1964 as a mixed hockey club, playing in an area called Whiteway. They used that as the name of the club. They played on a pitch rented from the local authority, but had no bar or other accommodation of their own. After a few years some of the men decided to form a men's team and after that a ladies' team was formed. Pressure for change emerged not just from the growth of new teams, but also from a deterioration in the standard of the public pitch. 'The pitches were disgusting and became dangerous. The grass was long. They didn't roll them. So we looked around for someone to adopt us,' said the secretary.

An obvious strategy for a club in such a position is to seek out cricket teams. This is because cricket clubs prefer to share a pitch with a hockey club. It creates less damage than football or rugby. There are also the benefits of shared maintenance and a likelihood that the bar and pavilion facilities will be better used and more profitable. It took five years of searching for Whiteway Hockey Club to find the Conwood Cricket Club, which was about three miles away. First contacts were successful, but Whiteway failed to realize at that stage how much the cricket club was tied in to the Conwood Folk Centre. Finally a deal was struck in which the hockey club would change its name to Conwood Hockey Club, and send a representative to the Sports Field Subcommittee of the Folk Centre and ensure that all its members joined the Folk Centre individually.

The motives of the cricket club for taking them on were gradually surmised by the hockey players. They believed that the cricket club first of all wanted a group to share the burden of maintaining the pitch, particularly by contributing to the cost of new equipment. They also felt that the cricket club wanted another group to help with the running of the bar and pavilion. Hockey members could see no altruism in the actions of cricket members. Soon an uneasy relationship developed: 'they bully us a lot, but we stand our ground. They thought they'd get a lot of equipment out of us, but it hasn't materialized,' said the secretary. In particular, the Sports Field Subcommittee persuaded the Folk Centre to purchase new rollers by agreeing that the hockey and cricket clubs would contribute £300 each, to be matched by the Folk Centre with £600. In the event the rollers purchased were, in the view of hockey members, totally unsuitable for anything other than maintenance of a cricket square. One member could not resist pointing out that the 'neutral' chairman of the subcommittee was in fact a long-standing member of the cricket team. The secretary had this to say about the later relationship: 'We're expected to attend "their" meetings. We've had problems with the Folk Centre committees. We're the new boys if you like. There's been some resentment from the cricket section.'

Despite such tensions the thrust by the hockey club to find a base was considerable. In their case this was because of a very strong feeling amongst the management at the time that they were as much a social club as a playing club and that social success demanded some form of physical base – a bar and pavilion. (Interestingly Redland Ladies' Hockey Club, a very successful local side that we also studied, managed to succeed without having their own premises, but this was because their definition of success was related exclusively to playing performance.)

At the time of our research the club had around thirty-five members, twenty women (always called 'ladies' in hockey circles and 'girls' at that particular club) and fifteen men. They ran four teams: one in the Sun Life League Western Division for men's outdoor teams, one in the Gloucestershire Country League for men's indoor teams, one ladies' team and one mixed team; the last two played in informal local circles rather than leagues.

Home games were played at Conwood, although indoor games required the *ad hoc* booking of a nearby sports centre. Three teams were, at the time, performing very badly; the outdoor league team being at the bottom of its division. The emphasis on pure enjoyment and the social side of the club came mostly from the older members who were, not surprisingly, also the longer established members whose original thrust had been towards social, mixed hockey rather than the very recent (and still resisted) leagues. It was also pointed out to us that several couples were members. (One couple had met first in the mixed team.) This social emphasis was connected by some members to a lack of concern for training, which took place (for all but the indoor team) only in the few weeks before the start of the season. These members contrasted this with the heavy stress on training for the indoor team and linked it to the fact that the indoor team was the only one doing well. Moreover, the stress on sociability was perhaps a factor in the club's inability to attract or hold on to new younger players for whom success on the pitch may well be more significant. They would not understand the secretary's statement that 'we can be beat 13 nil and can have a drink and laugh about it'.

It was not that there were too many social activities, merely that there were conflicting views about the importance of success on the field. Perhaps again this is a feature of age and marital status. The ladies' team were older: 'happy with one game every six or seven weeks... being married and that', as the secretary put it. 'The problem with ladies' hockey is that it's kids first and hockey second on a Saturday afternoon. If it carries on the way it is, there isn't going to be a ladies' team,' said the ladies' captain. The current men's (outdoor) captain represents one viewpoint on this issue generally: 'I enjoy a team game, a league game... the competitive aspect probably a bit more than the social aspect.' Many of the older members and the committee clearly realized that this dilemma existed. They simply could not see a solution. Almost all members lived in west Bristol and this makes it more difficult to attract a solid core of new east Bristol members, living close to the pitch.

As with many sports clubs, the team captains are also on the club's committee. In Conwood's case, both captains were very new and had to be persuaded to take on the role. Both captains felt that the presence on the pitch of senior members, in particular those who had been captains and were still occupying roles such as chairman and secretary, makes life very difficult for them. While these senior members were all 'fed up with doing the captaincy themselves, the majority of the team live in awe of the strong committee rather than me,' said the men's captain. He was also unaware of the prevailing view of these senior members in favour of the social dimension. According to the secretary, 'we accept that fact that we will never do well', so 'we just try to enjoy it'. The captain, on the other hand, felt that if results didn't improve, 'I'll start to assert my voice a little louder and make a few changes.'

Meanwhile, the ladies' captain felt thwarted in her attempts to try out new players: 'The girls' section is to a certain extent... I think the word is cliquey. It's a section that's played together for some years. They are mostly in the thirty to forty age bracket. We've discussed this at committee because at times we've felt we don't make new players welcome.'

Both captains also expressed confusion over persuading other players to take responsibility for arranging things like 'oranges, shirts and teas'. The previous captain (now secretary) felt that 'the men have always been good at doing jobs. In previous years captains have delegated responsibility', but the chairman felt that the current captain is shouldering the lot. The captain felt that if either the chairman or secretary were to ask players to help, they would immediately get a positive response, suggesting that he himself would not and that they cannot see the blockage.

The distinct impression which arises from all this is that committee meetings are rather unnecessary. Certainly the meeting we attended was run very much by the old guard, who then stayed behind after for a drink while the captains had to 'rush off'.

Our presentation of this cameo may suggest that dissent was rife within the club, even without the tensions arising from its relationship with the Folk Centre. We do not know why their link with the Folk Centre was eventually severed, nor whether they have yet found another venue or name. Yet our contact with this group, which was not one in which issues were glossed over, was very amicable and there was a strong feeling of friendliness and willingness to seek solutions. We hope the phoenix rises.

Matthews Morris Men

Most weekends through the summer, in Leicestershire villages and occasionally in the city, morris dancing groups – properly called 'sides' – can be seen performing at pubs and on open spaces. It is tempting to see this either as a meeting of eccentrics, or as an excuse for heavy drinking, even as an outdated male preserve. Such preconceptions shield what is in fact a complex and fascinating world, exemplified by the Matthews Morris Men. Theirs is a story not just of their own existence as a group but also of their continuing struggle – not always acrimonious – with what may seem an anachronism, a morris dancing 'establishment'.

The morris dancing establishment, of which Matthews Morris are not members, is called 'the Ring'. It is a federation or association of officially recognized morris sides from around the country, based around Cecil Sharp House in London, the home of the English Folk Dance and Song Society (EFDS). 'The Ring are like a secret society. They have a stringent set of rules. You've got to comply with them all before they'll let you in.' They demand a competent teacher (that is, approved by themselves), access to a set of books of standard dances, a constitution and some fairly standardized patterns of dancing. Until you are in the Ring you cannot get hold of the books of dances, that is, it is a rather good catch 22.

Matthews Morris originated in 1976 out of a folk dance group meeting at the St Matthews Centre in Leicester. On the admission of the deputy squire they 'had no traditional morris among us but wanted to have a go at it.' They persuaded a friend from a genuine morris side to come along informally and show them some dances after they had started to learn from books which they had acquired secretly. There was some talk of joining an existing group, but the nearest was in the doldrums and, according to the bagman, they felt they 'might lose their identity if they had gone in with another group as we already had our roots in other forms'. Actually they may also have been rather suspicious of the Ring and quite keen to subvert its influence. Their friend still comes in the winter months 'to put us right where we're going wrong', the squire added, 'we enjoy doing the dances the way he tells us to do them although he changes his mind sometimes.' There appear to be obligations about a balance between tradition and change – not necessarily shared by all in the Ring – that can be summed up by saying that it is a tradition to change. Recently, however, the EFDS have been trying to standardize, both to record changes and to allow what appears to be a more frequent sharing of dancing between sides. One basic tradition, related like many to particular towns or areas, is the Bampton tradition, one the Matthews Morris use quite a lot. Another feature of the Ring is their attitude to women: 'that's against the rules to have a lady musician . . . we'd be struggling to get in on that score as well.' Interestingly, however, it was women who kept the traditions going during the last war and there are now more women involved as dancers and some wholly female sides. One original member was very against any women joining the team and would not come for a year. Nevertheless, their musician (the wife of a dancer) is absolutely indispensable and the member concerned has now realized that they would get nobody else, so he has returned happily. Their independence from the national Ring is obviously a source of some pride. Not surprisingly, there was some resistance originally from the other side, especially because the objective is to dance in public, often by invitation, and they were on someone else's territory. As a result, according to one member, 'there were some very nasty remarks last year.'

Each group has its own informal territory and Matthews are still creating theirs. 'There was one pub that was visited by four groups in four consecutive weeks and they got a bit uppity. They are trying to concentrate on the north-east of the county. We had a bit of a conflict with the squire in the north-east. You're supposed to get in touch with the local squires and ask permission.'

They dance quite regularly now and usually make collections, though they are quick to point out that they don't go out to make collections. Recently they have consolidated their monies and been out for a dinner together. They rehearse through the winter – though they would happily admit that their meetings are as much to stay together as to practise. They rent a small hall at the St Matthews Centre (an obvious contact, given the folk dance link) and meet weekly. Most members – there are twelve – attend regularly, but one or two have occasional problems with shift work. There are seven of the original nine left, newcomers arriving either via the general folk scene or 'from cold'. One man only joined after driving his son to the society a few times. Within three or four weeks he felt reasonably confident, and is now very keen and goes to festivals with his family. He is self-employed, having been made redundant a few years ago, so he and his wife do barn dance calling for money.

Some new members leave quite quickly; others stay. One potential problem for a newcomer is the dress, although much of the costume can be made from everyday clothes. 'The bowler's the hardest thing to come by, but at the outset this is never forced.' The group is run very informally. There are traditional management roles, secretary (deputy squire), chairman (squire), treasurer (bagman). There is also a swordmaster, because they perform some sword dances on occasion. They hold an AGM after an evening practice: 'Because you need one annual meeting to overlook how you've done... it helps us to sort out what we've got in the bag, to air any grievances that people have ' (deputy squire). This reflects a clear wish to avoid formality: 'We're all friends, we all know each other and we don't feel there's a need for a constitution ' (deputy squire). It seems that part of the rather assertive independence from the Ring also hides a strong feeling about the seriousness of their activity. 'In the mainstream, there is a chauvinist, old-fashioned idea of getting out with the lads. None of our men here really like having a special evening out away from the family. I often think of us as odd, when you think of how morris men normally swig back the ale.'

The other local (Ring) side are almost too keen: 'They're trying to be perfect all the time and that's not our attitude. We've always been told, wherever we've been, that we always enjoy ourselves, which is what we're doing it for. Other groups, not a smile to be seen, even when they've finished ' (squire). Yet, according to the bagman, 'Some of our discipline is not very brilliant; not, that is, in practice. Maybe sometimes we don't concentrate as we should when we are practising, but on show you wouldn't fault us.' According to an ordinary member, 'There isn't really enough of a driving force behind the side. There's not really anybody in charge. The squire will not tell anybody what to do. Some members don't give a damn – they think they know everything and they don't.' However, the squire himself says that they require a lot of pushing, 'the majority are a bit apathetic. They want the team to carry on, but they don't want any more responsibilities. If I said I wasn't coming any more, I'm certain the team would fold up.'

Despite these contradictions, the group conveys a clear impression of friendly exchange and a sense that they all realize that different views will always coexist: 'It doesn't matter what we do, everybody laughs and jokes about it.'

Charnwood Aquarists' Society

The Charnwood Aquarists' Society has met, without interruption, since its inception in 1934. Its members are drawn from all parts of Leicester and some of the surrounding villages. Currently it has thirty-four full members, one junior and eight honorary members, its membership having almost halved during the last six years. Interestingly, while its membership has declined, its reputation as a society within aquarist circles has advanced considerably over the last few years. Its membership is strongly working class and, while all ages are represented, the bulk of its members are aged between twenty-five and forty.

Unlike many sports and hobbies, aquarism is not easily defined. Essentially it involves the keeping, breeding or showing of tropical fish. However, it is clear that widely different opinions are held by aquarists as to the nature of the true aquarist. The society's secretary is one of the many aquarists who likes keeping fish in ornamental community tanks. She does not breed fish nor is she particularly interested in competitive showing. Others in the club feel aquarism is really something which transcends this. According to the show secretary, 'most people keep fish almost as an ornament. When they come along to the club, they find how deep the hobby goes.' Nevertheless, even those who are very much engaged in competitive showing would not be regarded as true aquarists by some of their colleagues. As one member put it, 'You're never an aquarist until you've bred fish.' The show secretary buys most of his fish from London; he does not breed fish at all. However, he is aware that some club members dislike showing because they feel it does unnecessary harm to fish. The secretary does not object to showing some of her fish at club nights, but would not take her fish to shows around the country as she feels this is 'a bit cruel'.

Besides these differences in attitude, aquarists also differ in terms of the kind of fish they keep. Tropical fish fall into two main categories: 'live bearers', the most common family of which is the guppy, and 'egg bearers', the most common family of which is the cichlid. There are literally thousands of types of fish within each family. Guppies are small, move about in great shoals and breed with alarming regularity – club members sometimes referred to them as 'millions fish'. Cichlids are larger, more aggressive and sensitive. As a devotee put it, they are 'more for the connoisseur', requiring 'advanced parental care'. Whilst a few club members specialize in breeding one particular kind of fish, the major distinction is between club members whose prime interest lies with live bearers and those whose interest lies with egg bearers; there are in fact national live bearer and egg bearer clubs to which many society members have an overlapping affiliation.

The controversy surrounding the nature of aquarism is also fuelled by the presence of cold-water fish enthusiasts. The society has three members who are devoted to cold-water fish – goldfish, carp, etc. This presents the society with some cultural difficulties. As one member said, 'You can't go up and say "How's your goldfish?" to them, because to them it's Orandas and Shubs and that.' Whilst the society is generally very welcoming and friendly, groups such as these do tend to live in glorious isolation within the warm-water fish culture. Although his perception may not be shared by others in the club, a new member described this group as if they resembled a small minority ethnic group in a bewildered and slightly resistant host culture: 'What they say I translate over to the others, because the others can't really understand them.'

The society works very hard to relate to all the needs of its members and particularly at striking a balance between the competitive and non-competitive interests of its members. The club meets twice every month, the first meeting always including a competitive show of members' own fish. At the beginning of the year the show secretary prepares a programme of society table shows so that all the main categories of fish kept by club members (including cold-water fish) can be displayed competitively.

The table shows – 'a little contest between us selves' – takes place at the beginning of the evening. Judges are brought in from outside and fishes are assessed according to size, colour, condition and deportation. According to the new member we met, contestants may get extra marks for a 'well-behaved fish' and this can make all the difference, for although four prizes are awarded for each category, 'coming second, third or fourth is nothing, even though you get your certificate and that's handy to have.' The winner of the show is awarded a small but very fine looking wooden trophy. Given that the club has nine table shows every year, and each show consists of a competition within two separate categories of fish, eighteen trophies and fifty-four certificates are awarded each year, and this is without taking into consideration the society's big annual open show (in which aquarists all over the country compete), and its presentation ceremony. At each table show one or two judges will be brought in from outside and typically their expenses will amount to £25 or so. Table shows are therefore an expensive element of the club's activities, but there can be no doubting the centrality of them to the society's life.

Typically the first arrivals at a table show evening will be the competitors themselves, perhaps between five and eight club members. The fish are placed in small display tanks at the back of the meeting room and, as society members arrive, each in turn quietly and respectfully inspects the fish on display for anything up to twenty minutes. The meeting will cover a few items of club business while the judging is going on at the back of the room, then there will be a break for coffee followed by an announcement of the judges' decisions and presentation of awards. Finally, to round off the evening, there will be a quiz or a question-and-answer session.

The second meeting of each month consists of an invited speaker rather than table show. The society has some difficulty in obtaining enough speakers to fill the year's programme. Even those that are booked sometimes fail to turn up. The club undoubtedly has a number of experts in its own midst but 'a lot of people just won't get up because they think they'd make a fool of themselves'. Nevertheless, according to the secretary, the society has a few members 'who are very well up – know all the Latin names that you need to know.' These few experts carry much of the responsibility for organizing events and presenting the club's image to the broader aquarist environment. It is not that the rest of the members have no expertise, rather they appear to be much more unsure about the adequacy of the knowledge and skill they have. Class may be a factor here. To circumvent this problem the society makes deliberate use of quizzes and question-and-answer sessions as a way of encouraging all members to contribute. At one meeting we attended, the show secretary asked the members present if any would like to act as speakers during the coming year and was met by an embarrassed silence. Only a few minutes later a few new members were encouraged to put to the meeting some questions they had raised informally over coffee. The discussion that followed continued for almost half an hour with many club members holding forth on issues such as the aetiology of certain kinds of aquatic fungus for several minutes at a time.

Average attendances at society meetings is currently around twenty-five, slightly up on last year. The club is the best known in

Leicester and is the only one listed in the city council's information guide. There are at least three other aquarist societies in Leicester, but some of them clearly have a different kind of appeal. According to the show secretary, the New Parks Estate club is very much based on that estate. 'It is very much a family affair where there's always a large amount of children and it always seems very disorganized.' The secretary discovered the society about three and a half years ago quite by accident. She became a regular attender because 'You get more information, the sort of knowledge people pass on, rather than just from reading.' About a year ago her tie with the club became much closer when she became secretary: 'I only joined up socially and I got landed with the job because nobody else would do it.' The new member we spoke to discovered the club at its marquee at the annual Abbey Park Show in Leicester. He came to a couple of meetings and borrowed a book, did not return for a long time but when he did he was pleasantly surprised. 'After a year, they knew me. So from there I thought, right, I'll join just to see how I can get on.' By the end of last year he had sold most of his fish, having become interested in cage birds. Nevertheless, at the AGM of the club in January he was asked if he would be willing to take responsibility for running the raffle (which is conducted every club night) 'so I thought, right, I've got a reason to stick to the club now'. The show secretary came to the club about four years ago, having moved up to Leicester from London where he had been an active member of the Sudbury Club, one of the most famous in the country. He arrived in Leicester just at the time when the society was considering running its own first open show and was co-opted immediately on to the show subcommittee.

The club works very hard at welcoming new members. New members arrived at the two meetings we attended and on both occasions great efforts were made by all present to engage them in conversation. If the newcomer is a novice, older members will often give them some fish and others might sell them equipment very cheaply. The society buys fish food and equipment in bulk which it then sells to its membership. Visiting speakers often bring fish with them to sell and members sell and barter fish between themselves and auctions of equipment and books, etc., are also held on a regular basis. Despite this, most society members still rely heavily on commercial dealers, even though their prices tend to be exorbitant.

The society has undergone a number of important changes over the last few years, changes which were both the result and the cause of tensions within the club. As a result of these changes a number of long-standing members have been squeezed off the committee to be replaced by younger members. Opinions vary as to the main cause of this change. One member highlighted a controversy surrounding a particular club rule: 'We had a riot about the five points.' The show secretary referred to the decision to organize an open show. Clearly a number of controversies had arisen.

The 'five-point rule' controversy refers to a recent attempt to alter a long-standing club rule whereby each club member is awarded five points for each meeting attended. At the end of the year, attendance points are added to points gained by each member at the table shows and the individual with the highest tally is declared aquarist of the year and is presented with the society silver bowl. The rule was introduced many years ago because, as one member put it, 'Some can't be bothered to go to the discussion, but only want to bring fish for the shows.' The year before, everyone had expected the silver bowl to be won by a young woman; however, when the points were added up, her attendance points were very low and the bowl went to someone else. The woman complained and the controversy blew up. Basically the younger members were against the five-point ruling because it discriminated against people like mothers and shiftworkers whose attendance was affected by factors beyond their control. According to the new member, 'now we've got new blood in the camp, we don't want it'. The change was resisted fiercely by older members, particularly the president. A compromise was hatched at this year's AGM and members can now keep their five points if they give notice of their absence to the secretary, so long as they do not attend only table show evenings. Despite their differences with other club members, the president and his wife are highly respected by all club members, the kind of 'grandparents' of the society.

The controversy surrounding the open show began when some members formed a small subcommittee to work on plans for the society to run its own national event. Open shows are a key event in the aquarist calendar. Each year individual societies organize their own shows, typically lasting two or three days and involving several hundreds of entries from all over the country. Competitions are held between all the major classes of fish and the host club presents all of the trophies. 'I presented one for a male guppy' (secretary). There is also a competition for the best fish in the show; besides receiving a coveted 'Best in Show' award, this fish is then eligible for the 'Champion of Champions' show held annually at Bellevue, Manchester – the Crufts of the fish world. According to the present show secretary, individual clubs that run their own open shows are ensured a national reputation. Some of the older members within Charnwood were very much against the idea of the open show, feeling that it was certain to lose money. The show subcommittee, however, got larger and larger as more and more members became interested in the idea, until the majority of the club committee was on the sub-committee. The first show was indeed a financial failure, but in all other respects it was a great success. Older members helped considerably with their expertise and contacts and judges were organized from all over the country. The society hired the St Matthews Centre in Leicester for the weekend of the show. They arranged their own catering, organized their own publicity, and produced and presented their own trophies. The following year the show only made a £50 loss and it was hoped that they would make a small profit the year after. The society now has a fast growing national reputation and the confidence of society members in their own organizing ability has grown considerably.

A third recent controversy has focused on changes in the society's normal activities. Until this year the society met monthly and meetings would combine a table show with an invited speaker. It was felt that monthly meetings inhibited greater member involvement, so a decision was taken to meet bi-monthly – again against the advice of the old guard. The secretary described this move as a little experiment 'to see if we can get members more interested'. The change has encouraged the management committee of the club to conduct all its business openly on table show evenings, the idea being to increase the sense of involvement of all club members in society business.

The management committee consists of nine members including the chairman, secretary, treasurer and show secretary. It is elected annually at the January AGM. 'If you don't want to do anything, keep away that night ' (secretary). There is no gulf between 'managers' and a passive membership; everyone seems to put in quite a lot of work, if not on day-to-day activities then on specific projects like the open show or the Abbey Park Show. The impression one gets is that whilst the society was certainly larger ten years ago, its membership was more passive than it is now.

Social activities in the club are important but not paramount. The society holds two or three dances a year organized by the younger members. They are well attended, discothèque affairs, but interestingly the vast bulk of those attending are not club members – they tend to be youngsters who like a good disco. The society makes quite a bit of money out of these dances and this seems to be their main function. The society organizes two social functions for its own members: in the summer an annual presentation evening, usually combined with skittles or something and 'a Christmas outing which is a sort of thank you for the effort over the year . . . a slap up meal and dance', as the show secretary put it.

The Federation of British Aquarist Societies is an important parent body. 'It is like being in a union, I suppose. It tells you all the regional whys and wherefores,' said the secretary. It produces its own magazine informing aquarists of events and shows, it trains judges, and so on. The FBAS, however, is very much a federation, power remaining with the local associations (which should not be regarded as branches of the FBAS). Perhaps the most important function concerns judging. Whilst a local aquarist can become accepted as a class C judge and may join regional judges' panels servicing table shows, to be a judge at an open show requires proper training. Aspirant judges have to go away on weekend training courses and, subject to passing a test, may then become a class B judge. Class B judges are in great demand. Within the society both the show secretary and the treasurer are reckoned to be of this standard, but neither have put themselves forward for training because both work Saturdays when class B judges are in most demand.

The only other element of the society's context worth mentioning is their relationship with the city council. Other than the fact that they use city council premises for their meetings (the St Matthews Centre) they have virtually no involvement with the local authority. The one exception is during the city's Abbey Park Show where the city council provide the society with a small marquee and all the necessary materials for them to mount a big public display. The club put a lot of effort into the display but, except for a raffle, are not allowed to raise any money from it. Nevertheless they have been committed to doing something for the Abbey Park Show for many years. It helps them to maintain their Leicester-wide profile and gains them quite a few new members.

Chapter 3

Mutual aid in leisure

It is an interesting fact that people will join together to form groups around anything which provides the slightest opportunity for organization. Of all the activities we encountered, there are perhaps just two – cookery and do-it-yourself – around which clubs or associations do not appear to have been built (perhaps because both of these are home-centred activities). Virtually every other leisure activity we have so far encountered that appears to be an essentially individual pursuit – for example, collecting things, gardening, wine-making, drawing – also generates a self-organized, collective form. Here we would like to make a distinction between collective forms of leisure activity which occur in the context of self-run groups and those occurring in day or evening classes; only the former can be properly considered as forms of self-organization. However, as we shall see later, the boundary between such groups and classes may often be a very nebulous one. There are also 'fraternities'.* The best known example of these is probably train-spotters, but their 'collectivity' is clearly of a different order to that of a group with a bounded and relatively stable membership. They are, however, strongly self-organized. Nevertheless, the distinctions are useful and our essential focus will generally be upon groups, not classes or fraternities.

The sheer range and scale of leisure activities in which people engage during their spare time is a remarkable but little understood phenomenon. Consider the following activities around which, to our certain knowledge, local clubs, societies and associations have been formed:

Basketball	Table tennis
Old-time dancing	Skittles
Chess	Beekeeping
Cats	Meditation
Aerobics	Antiques
Orchestras	Hockey
Football	Toy dogs
Lapidary	Aquarism

*We have been unable to find any suitable non-sexist term to replace 'fraternity'.

Fishing
Morris dancing
Tennis
Flower arranging
Bridge
Gardening
Fuchsias
Windsurfing
Railway preservation
Allotments
War games
Cricket
Wine
Philately
Photography
Horse riding
Canoeing
Women's Institutes
Microlights
Harmoniums
Netball
Ballroom dancing
Guitars
Whist
Keep fit
Judo
Wrestling
Athletics
Brass bands
Caving
Handball
Darts
Metal detectors
Volleyball
Parascending
Orienteering
Rat fancying
Computer games
Point-to-point
Family histories
Lacrosse
Climbing
Local history
Industrial archaeology

Hang-gliding
Numismatism
Naturalism
Snooker
Mums and toddlers groups
Clocks
Practical conservation
Vintage motor cycles
Military modelling
Modern sequence dance
Computers
Rowing
Film and video
Folk dance
Wives' groups
Squash
Sub-aqua
Sailing
Weight-lifting
Motor scooters
Handicrafts
Bird watching
Choirs
Slimming
Boxing
Aikido
Drama
Light opera
Lace making
Softball
Macrame
Yoga
Bowls
Gymnastics
Shove-ha'penny
Upholstery
Silk-screen printing
Oil painting
Rifle and pistol shooting
Model railways
Cycling
Whippets
Dress-making
Swimming

Skating

Mouse fancying

Leek growing

Caged birds

Aero modelling

Pigeon racing

Canal preservation

Model boats

It is difficult, if not impossible, to classify much of this activity – is ice-dancing, for example, a sport or an art-form? Is photography an art or a hobby? Nevertheless we can try to allocate particular activities to one of four categories: sports, arts, crafts, hobbies. Obviously some groups cannot be placed in these categories; for example, youth groups, mothers and toddlers clubs or Women's Institutes.

Sports

This is probably the easiest category to grasp, covering many well-known activities from football to archery, handball to pistol shooting. However, a plethora of new sports – hang-gliding and softball, for example – have emerged only recently in Britain and many new developments have occurred within existing sports, such as swimming, where 'swim-jogging', synchronized swimming, etc., have all appeared during the last few years. Within all sports, however, major differences can be observed in terms of their organization (teams are essential in football but unimportant in pistol shooting), size of club (400–600 for swimming, twenty-four for badminton) and form of training (whereas the 'coach' is essential to swimming, gymnastics or judo instruction, training is pursued informally among peers in shooting, angling or snooker).

Arts

This covers painting, drama, music, dance and so forth. Within each of these a host of different activities take place. 'Dance', for example, covers everything from Scottish country, Northumbrian, morris and square-dancing, through to modern ballroom, old-time, ballet, 'break' and disco dancing.

Crafts

This term includes a variety of pursuits from lapidary to weaving. Almost without exception the products from craft groups are individual, although members may work together to prepare a set display or exhibition. The boundary between craft and hobby can become hazy, as with aquarism or military modelling, and some activities – especially photography – can be thought of as equally art, craft or hobby.

Hobbies

This includes a vast range of activities such as rearing and breeding (insects, plants and animals); collecting (clocks, stamps); accounting (train-spotting, bird-watching); modelling, gaming, preserving, restoring, etc. The range here is considerable and one hobby group would probably never imagine themselves to have anything in common with another. It also becomes less easy to distinguish anything resembling training (which might occur in a class) because it is assumed by participants that the whole process of taking part is in itself educational.

Hobby activity also appears to rely more on peer-group support than on external display, so its products are more likely to be generated for fellow enthusiasts than the general public.

Why do enthusiasts join groups?

First of all, there are a large number of activities which are by their very nature collective, for example, team games, drama, folk dance, bands and orchestras. Secondly, free association would appear to be necessary for certain leisure activities where the required facilities can only be collectively provided. Thus, for most individuals, the cost of establishing a personal shooting range would be prohibitive. Similarly, a number of anglers join fishing clubs because, in many areas nowadays, access to adequate stretches of water is extremely difficult. One joins a club to gain access to a particular gravel pit or part of a river. For similar reasons, many inland yachtsmen join yachting clubs, snooker players join snooker clubs and so forth. Of course, such facilities can be provided by other forms of organization, public or commercial. Thirdly, competition is another factor leading to interaction and forms of social organization. Very often competition may lead to the organization of an activity, even though competitors may never meet each other. This is the case, for example, with inter-club rifle shooting competitions or some photographic competitions.

Clearly, free association is a necessary condition for the performance of many leisure activities, but there are others for which it appears to be an entirely discretionary strategy. Why, for example, do aquarists or gardeners form themselves into clubs, when major aspects of their hobby can be pursued quite satisfactorily alone at home? Again, we would suggest three reasons. First, leisure groups provide a vehicle through which social exchange can take place; people with common enthusiasms can exchange information, provide each other with informal guidance and training, trade anecdotes, etc. This is linked closely to the immersion of enthusiasts within their own particular sub-cultures. Secondly, groups provide opportunities for creating collective rather than individual products – for instance, most of the best model railways to be seen at exhibitions throughout the country are club layouts, often the product of thousands of person-hours' activity. Thirdly, groups provide opportunities for making friends and meeting people, suggesting that the substantive activity itself may be of secondary importance. Even the most competitive of sports clubs will tend to have a highly developed social side to the club's activity. As we shall see, for many organizations this purely social dimension to their existence may not be quite legitimate to discuss openly but may shape their final identity far more than the nature and rules of their ostensible leisure activity. If this is true, it provides a serious challenge to the traditional, 'functional' model of leisure planning described in the Introduction.

The scale of self-organized activity

We have considered the range of activities. What about the scale? In Kingswood we located around 300 groups. Our search was by no means comprehensive but, assuming an average membership of around ninety, this produced 28,500 people active in the area. This would seem a very high percentage of a total population of around 85,000 (although it should be remembered that some were members of two or three groups, and that some group members came from outside this area). Only 37 per cent involved sporting activities. There were, for example, five photography societies, eight drama societies, four chess clubs and five gardening clubs. The total includes just over 100 'multi-function' groups, many of which contained additional single-purpose clubs (for example, youth football teams, pensioner choral groups) which were not counted separately in our estimates. Furthermore, many single-purpose sports clubs fielded several teams – some soccer clubs, for example, contained up to four separate teams, each competing in different divisions of the same league.

Our research also suggests that over half of the groups in Kingswood had been running for more than fifteen years, many for much longer. Downend Cricket Club, for example, started in 1893, Frampton Cotterell Badminton Club in 1945, North Bristol Cribbage League in 1946, Severn Road Club (Cycling) in 1932 and so on.

We have quoted this example because it is typical of what one might call 'middle England'. In our other sampled area of north-east Leicester activity was not so widespread and mostly fairly recent. Here a preliminary survey located 228 groups (the population of this wedge of north-east Leicester was approximately 68,000) with an average membership of about fifty-five. Many of the same activities occurred as in Kingswood, but sport tended to be more of the indoor variety, probably reflecting the lack of outdoor facilities common to most city environments, and martial arts appeared to be more popular, specifically within the large Asian community. Although north-east Leicester possessed some very old clubs (Belgrave Amateur Boxing Club, 1947, West Humberstone Allotment Society, 1918) there was a much greater preponderance of newly formed (post-1970) clubs here than in Kingswood (about 66 per cent as opposed to 40 per cent). To illustrate scale further, we could consider one community college in north-east Leicester. A by no means comprehensive tally of the groups in existence at this one centre would reveal two adult and one youth football clubs, one largely Asian cricket club, a gardening club, a lapidary society, an Irish society, a community orchestra, a photography club, an audio-visual club, a junior gym club and two yoga clubs.

So far, however, we have considered the scale of activity in terms of the number of groups functioning in particular localities or attached to particular community centres. Another way of considering the scale of activity is to focus upon aspects of its 'depth' – that is, how much of one particular activity occurs in a given area. We will use football as an example, largely because our impression is that it is the most popular collective leisure activity. We would estimate that well over 3,000 men* are involved as players in amateur football in the Leicester area on Saturdays alone. The Leicester City league has eight divisions with fourteen teams in each, the Leicester Mutual League has four divisions with fourteen teams in each and, in addition, many Leicester clubs play in either the Leicester and District League, the Leicestershire Combination or, if they are of a very high standard, in the Leicestershire Senior League. Moreover, some of the teams, particularly those in the Senior League with their own ground or smaller teams who draw their members from one ethnic group or identifiable community, are themselves quite well supported. The primary unit, however, is not the team but the club.

---

* We have no evidence of women's football in Leicester.

Each club will have its own group of usually non-playing organizers; the key figure being the club secretary. Many clubs also have *team* managers and there appears to be a growing fashion towards the use of team coaches, even at the lowest levels of amateur football. Virtually all secretaries, managers, coaches, etc., are older players who have 'hung up their boots'. We have also, on occasion, met a secretary or coach who has never in fact played serious club football!

As we shall see later, the collective and self-organized nature of leisure is not limited to the level of individual groups. A further aspect of 'depth' is that many groups are themselves the bedrock of still broader and more complex forms of social organization. Wherever one finds individual groups, one is almost certain also to find federations, leagues, associations and so forth of a local, regional, national, even international nature. The world of photography illustrates this well.

The club we studied in Kingswood also shared some of its members informally with the major Bristol group. It is formally registered with the Western Counties Photographic Federation, an amalgam of ninety clubs in an area from Gloucestershire to Cornwall. The WCPF arranges some of its own exhibitions and competitions but also supports those run by individual clubs. It is through the WCPF that the local network of judges is organized. There are two levels of judging – one for club (that is regional/local) competitions and another for federation and 'open' competitions. The WCPF has thirty-one approved judges and, as well as sitting at home judging those photographs sent to them, they also have to travel, often long distances, to explain and justify their choices at exhibitions.

The clubs, through the WCPF, are also members of the Photographic Alliance of Great Britain. This organization controls the list of approved judges, has a list of recommended lecturers (and very precise rules regarding payment of expenses), arranges a loans service of quality prints and slides and offers good insurance arrangements. Each of the twelve local federations (for example, WCPF) is then responsible, in turn, for hosting the inter-federation competition. Finally, through the alliance, there are links to an international network; the Fédération Internationale de l'Art Photographique.

Who participates?

In illustrating both range and scale of activity, there is a danger of implying that men and women, old people and children, the disabled, ethnic groups and all social classes participate in these activities to the same degree and in the same ways. It should be obvious that this is not true but our own experience during the research would also lead us to reject the opposite argument – that there are always major, and often worrying, divergencies. Perhaps the most significant variations occur along lines of gender, race and class, so we shall deal first with these before some brief comments on age and disability.

In relation to gender, some simple facts are useful. Of those groups replying to our questionnaire, forty-five were exclusively for, or likely to be dominated by, men, and thirty-one for women. However, fifty-five were mixed and these results show little variation between Kingswood and Leicester. Recent campaigns have focused on leisure participation by women, but the assumption of lower levels of female involvement have emerged primarily from information about sports. Our numbers are too small to allow more detailed analysis but we would suspect that, while it is probably true that women participate less in sport, they are very well represented in arts, crafts and hobbies. Such propositions about participation also begin to seem less clear cut if one considers our purely anecdotal knowledge of the type of leisure organization which women join.

Our brief coverage of multi-function groups shows the number and variety of these specifically for women and it did appear to us that women often prefer not merely a woman-only group but also one not tied to a specific activity. Perhaps this is a reflection of a lesser concern for competitiveness and substantive activity, more a concern for social support. Such arguments may also apply to another phenomenon noticed only briefly in our work. It appeared to us that many women also prefer involvement in classes rather than formal groups, yet such involvement was not always as passive recipients; rather, many classes for women became 'proto-groups' in which there was less emphasis on the 'teacher' and more on reciprocation and sharing, (for example, keep fit). One further reason for women's involvement with classes is almost certainly that such classes are far less continuously demanding than involvement in groups. Classes start and finish at set times and on set dates; no (or little) member organization is required and to miss one week is almost expected rather than a surprise – all far more appropriate to a woman occupying a traditional role at home.

The interplay between ethnicity and leisure participation was more elusive. Most crafts and hobbies appear to remain largely within the culture which first generated them; we know of no black railway modellers or white Asian volleyball players. (Asian volleyball is quite different from its European namesake.) It is not surprising to find most environmental groups being white, Anglo-Saxon dominated because of the roots of such concerns in long-term history rather than the more recent multi-cultural dimension. Within sports, however, the interlinking is far more fluid, although we noticed a general trend for ethnic groups to 'club together', even in activities dominated by no single group.[1] Some variations are, however, clear and informative. In Leicester (our only source in the absence of a mixed community in Kingswood) cricket appeared to be a highly integrated activity, the majority of clubs containing players from the black and Asian communities as well as local whites. Football, however, was very highly segregated with many teams comprised solely of one ethnic group. We also came across a number of multi-function groups specifically for a single ethnic group and usually also for men or women only. Such examples are, of course, to be expected within, for example, Muslim communities. In summary, however, it did seem to us that ethnic minority groups are less likely to become involved in or form the type of group we are describing here. This cannot be taken to mean that they do not find outlets elsewhere or even that alternative forms of organization are culturally preferred. We certainly experienced no direct exclusion on ethnic grounds, but it no doubt exists, hence limiting choice. There are clearly some important issues here for further work.

In considering class, some of the above issues reappear, with the same provisos about our coverage. First, as with gender and ethnic variations, one expects to find class variation in choice of activity – croquet and whippets are two everyday stereotypes. This we found, though to a much less dramatic degree than we expected. There was a tennis club in Kingswood; none emerged in Leicester. There was a boxing club in Leicester; none emerged in Kingswood. There were folk dance groups, flower arranging and gymnastics in each. Secondly, in terms of simple quantity of participation, while the crude numbers in both areas were surprising, it is probably also true that the participation in Leicester was lower. This would have been seen even more dramatically a few years ago in Leicester, before the intervention of the Urban Programme, because a large number of current groups were formed as a direct result of that initiative. Thirdly we could find nothing in the varying patterns between Leicester and Kingswood to indicate less involvement by working-class people in formal, structured, organized groups in preference for more open and less ordered settings. Fourthly, we did, however, find purely anecdotal evidence that problems of unemployment and poverty can affect participation inasmuch as less disposable income is available for equipment, kit, materials and so forth.

In terms of age, there was little to report that is not self-evident. Few pensioners play football and no young women attend luncheon clubs. Yet many clubs have members who are ex-players or were at one time major participants, but who now involve themselves either just socially or in organization – and are often indispensable for that. At the same time many multi-function groups for the elderly contain extremely passive members who have never been involved in self-organization before. If age does not appear to act as an inhibitor, neither does youth; we came across many groups which either had no lower age limits or which had them but did not invoke them. As mentioned before, there were also a large number of groups run quite specifically for children – gymnastics, karate and so forth – and most of these tended to be run by someone equivalent to an evening class teacher.

For disabled people the picture is very varied. Naturally many hobby, art and craft clubs can and do welcome disabled people, while others no doubt make it clear that they are not welcome. Participation in sport is more problematic, although we found people involved in archery and snooker. We located only one sports club specifically for the disabled (an angling club in Kingswood), perhaps because most provision takes the form of sessions and clubs run by local authorities or interest groups. In both Kingswood and Leicester we spoke to people involved in running groups for the disabled, and those to whom we spoke – themselves disabled – offered strong views on charitable provision, even on the Physically Handicapped/Able-Bodied Clubs which were established specifically to break down barriers. The impression was that they would prefer either true integration in everyday groups or to have their own groups run entirely by themselves.

In summary, then, although the picture is probably not as lop-sided as many would suggest, it does seem that women, blacks, Asians (and other ethnic groups), the elderly, the disabled and working-class people do participate less, in different types of group and in somewhat different activities. Partly because of our sample numbers, and partly because we do not consider such variations dramatic enough in relation to our prime focus, we do not deal distinctly with such variations elsewhere in the book except briefly on occasion. However, later chapters should enable the interested reader to begin to generate some personal interpretations for why the patterns described above might occur and whether they are inevitable.

Terms

We have tried here to convey some idea of the myriad groups involved in leisure activity, of the range and depth of activity which they cover, and of the leagues, federations, etc. which build from this bedrock. What concepts can we employ to bring some order and meaning to this vast and superficially random area of activity? The conventional academic or professional answer to this question would be to invoke the title we used ourselves at the outset of our research work. One could suggest (as did our research clients at the outset) that we are focusing on the 'Voluntary Sector in Leisure and Recreation'. Without getting embroiled in a tedious semantic argument, we wish to claim that this title is actually very inappropriate, even dangerous in its bearing on the territory we are beginning to describe.

Consider the word *voluntary*. In our conversations with group members, we met very few people who would accept that their involvement in their group constitutes any form of *volunteering*. Indeed, some would vehemently deny that they are volunteers because, even if they are virtually full-time organizers of large groups, their motivation is primarily that of personal pleasure in their activity rather than one of offering philanthropic effort and service to others. (We are aware that we may be dealing here with stereotypical notions of 'voluntary', etc.).

Next consider the word *sector*. This implies some coherence, shared sense of identity and common aims. Our conversations with members lead us to think that it is inconceivable to imagine bringing together a drama group with a rifle club, a folk dance society and a military modelling club. Indeed, we found that even a local Sports Council had difficulty sustaining corporate interest amongst its members. One can consider the general position of this 'sector' in leisure as compared to the voluntary sector in welfare. For the latter (as Wolfenden stated[2]) one part of their role is to fill the gaps left by the public sector, and hence they can create little action-space of their own, independent of formal provision. In the world of leisure, the relationship is the opposite: it is the public sector which has to try to fill the gaps and provide the 'enabling' which permits the many distinct clubs and societies to continue. If we were to be slightly cynical, we would suggest that the use of the construct 'voluntary sector in leisure' is a process generated by those in power (who generally have a simple functional model of leisure) with the intention of bringing a diverse territory into some form of order to make it manageable. Without a sense of the cultural richness of the varied groups, and of their independence from certain socio-economic forces, one is bound to reduce complexity to a 'sector'. We are clearly hinting here that – perhaps not deliberately – the actions of some agencies involved with the world of leisure are in danger of reducing this cultural richness, of 'colonialising' a diverse territory. We return to this issue in our final chapter.

Finally, let us look at the word *leisure*. Many have struggled with

definitions of this odd term. A crude Marxist analysis would place
leisure as a superstructural element, residual to underlying socio-
economic forces and an indicator of the alienation of the populace
from work and from constructive political action. For those from the
liberal tradition, leisure may not have such rigid links to other areas
of social and economic life, nor is it a territory manipulated
deliberately by those in power to pacify the proletariat. It is, however,
a spare-time, individualist activity rather than a locus for social
cohesion and change. Underlying both definitions, there is also that
strong functionalist tradition which sees any group activity as merely
a means to an end and denies that involvement with a group can offer
significant personal and social benefits in its own right.[3] Neither
perspective construes leisure as the site for relatively autonomous
forms of collective activity which play a significant role in the overall
cultural life of a society.

We feel that the issue of the language we use is crucial. The phrase
'the voluntary sector in leisure and recreation' is a misleading one.
While we can offer no ideal alternative, the term we use – despite its
own limitations – is 'communal leisure'. We must now describe those
aspects of the groups constituting communal leisure which serve to
demonstrate our object – if it is not a voluntary sector. We would
argue that the majority of these groups are mutual-aid organizations
whose ostensible prime purpose is a leisure or recreation activity.
They are collectivities which are self-organized, productive and which,
by and large, consume their own products. This is why they may be
more than merely 'leisure groups' – because there is probably no
other setting in our society where people can freely come together to
produce something outside the market economy, primarily for
consumption by themselves or their friends and neighbours.

It should be obvious that all the activities listed thus far are
collective – even if the outcomes are still individual – and that the
majority are self-organized. Groups organized as classes are usually
arranged, managed and dependent upon a few people. These groups
are often primarily for children (for example, gymnastics) and may
have just one teacher who does not see herself or himself, or is not
seen, as a true 'member' of the group. Within such 'class groups',
relationships between organizers and 'organized', teachers (or
instructors) and the 'taught', begin to resemble the provider/client
relationship which is typical of so many voluntary organizations
engaged in health and social services spheres.

In our experience leisure groups (as opposed to classes or 'class
groups') vary considerably in terms of the involvement of members in
the group's organization. We have encountered local drama societies
where virtually all of the thirty or so members are involved in the

organization of the society in some way or another, where seats on the management committee are closely contested at each AGM, and so on. When questioned about this, some members wondered whether this might have something to do with a sense of the dramatic applied to the organization of the society itself. At the opposite extreme we have encountered some pensioners' clubs where interest in organiza-tion was so weak that quorate AGMs were obtained by a deliberate policy of springing the AGM upon an unsuspecting membership who had turned up for a quite different kind of meeting!

Our experience of the mutual aid form of organization therefore suggests to us that relationships between 'organizers' and 'the organized' can assume a variety of forms which only rarely include the fully participatory model of maximum involvement of all members in all decisions. However, in no way does this undermine the sense of the organization being a self-organized collectivity. Even if the organizers are returned unopposed to their posts year after year, there is still a crucial difference between the nature of the organizations they run and those typical of, say, the voluntary welfare area. The essential difference lies in the way in which the members perceive the organizers. Is the organization done 'by some of us, for all of us' or is it performed 'by them, for us'? Only the former is an instance of the mutual aid form and as soon as one begins to speak in terms of the latter one has gone beyond mutual aid into the realm of 'servicer/serviced' relationships where it is legitimate to speak of 'voluntary' organizations, 'volunteers' and perhaps 'sec-tors'.

The key point, however, is not that these two different perceptions hide otherwise similar relationships, but the very quality of relationships between members of any mutual aid group is one of a crucially different nature. The basis of mutual aid is reciprocity, to the extent that relationships – essentially the exchange of effort and involvement – are governed by a very loose concept of 'give and take'. A small hockey club may be watched by only a handful of people, but these are almost certain to be committee members or ex-players. While the club may be the organizational product of these 'spectators', such effort only has real value when reciprocated (in a different form) by the players on the pitch. (One can even add that the outcomes are equally dependent upon the visiting team!) It is this aspect of the quality of the exchange relationship which leads us to use the apparently odd terms 'production' and 'consumption'. Clearly many groups *produce* something. For gardeners this is obvious, similarly modellers, artists and photographers. If one views a play or an exhibition as a 'production', it becomes possible to construe a netball game or a badminton match as a production also.

In other words, in communal leisure people come together to engage in a specific type of productive activity, whether it be individual (to produce a necklace), corporate (some scenery), tightly specified (a football cup match) or rather open-ended (a gardening show). Furthermore, there is a sense in which group members see the overall identity and character of their group as a product also. Almost any group we encountered was able to locate itself in terms of its character in relation to others and each was quite proud of its balance between substantive (for example, competitive) aspects and the more diffuse social factors. If we look now at *consumption*, a fuller meaning becomes available to the idea of reciprocity, because the essential distinguishing factor is that the products we have described are, in mutual aid groups, consumed by the producers themselves. The consumption does not have to be direct and immediate; thus after much preparation a drama group will present its production to an audience. We have, however, noticed that the majority of small drama societies generate audiences comprised almost entirely of friends, relatives and local residents – another form of 'us' rather than 'them'. There are certainly some extremes in which all the products of a group are exclusively for consumption by group members – perhaps a small flower-arranging group with no teacher as such, no exhibitions and no contact with wider flower-arranging circles. There are, however, many groups, probably the majority, in which the products are ostensibly available for public consumption (on a park playing field or at a military modelling exhibition, for example), but where the only 'consumers' are the participants and their peers (military modellers from other clubs) or ex-participants (as in the hockey club). It is probably even true that the absence of the general public, far from demeaning the value of what is presented, actually enhances its value because comment or criticism is a reaction by recognized peers. It is this important dimension of self-consumption which utterly transforms the meaning of the activity from that experienced in commercialized or professionalized forms of leisure.

In describing what we consider to be the key elements which serve to distinguish communal leisure from other areas of activity – collectivity, self-organization, production for self-consumption, mutual aid – we are aware that we are offering 'ingredients'. They do not, however, of themselves adequately characterize or explain the remarkable resilience and often assertive independence of the world of communal leisure which we experienced in our work. We will find ourselves returning frequently to this elusive aspect which we shall call 'identity' and which is far more than just a mere addition of ingredients. It is ultimately this aspect of the many groups which is both precious and yet at the same time most threatened.

Chapter 4

Leisure sub-cultures

Sometimes during our research we felt almost like anthropologists studying unfamiliar, isolated societies with their own languages, rule-systems and conventions. We encountered 'twitchers', 'pot-hunters', 'scratch-builders', 'live-bearers', 'callers' and so forth. We experienced the hushed reverence of a photographic exhibition, the fervent commitment of a volleyball team, the rituals of the post-match drinking of football players and the incomprehensible patterns of a military modelling evening. It was not simply that, to many participants, this wider social setting was as important as the activity itself, but that the values and traditions implicit in any activity linked quite directly to wider values. Thus lapidarists talked of the excitement of meeting a fellow enthusiast on holiday and being able to 'talk stone', and we ourselves were frequently assumed to be initiates of the activity's sub-culture, to know its language and indeed share many values other than those of the central activity. It was almost as if being a morris dancer spoke for sets of values in relation not just to dancing but also home, work, attitudes to children, even political views. This experience led us to adopt then extend a conclusion reached by others that we need 'a notion of leisure which incorporates culture as a series of constructive meanings and not simply as the satisfaction of leisure needs or gratifications'.[1]

While accepting a cultural perspective, we feel it is essential to recognize the many very different forms of cultural phenomena expressed by groups through their activities and therefore feel it is useful to think of the existence of distinct leisure sub-cultures. Our discovery of such patterns may have come through our contact with individual groups, but sub-culture is the activity itself and we will illustrate shortly the many ways in which different activities incorporate and contribute to sub-cultural variation. Thus an individual can be a 'member' of a sub-culture though not involved in any formal group – train-spotters are a good example. Equally, the external manifestations of any sub-culture come not just through its constituent clubs and societies, but also through leagues, federations, magazines, shows, contests and so forth. Sub-cultures can therefore be seen to occupy an intermediate position, existing in the space between the individual or club engaged in a leisure activity and the wider social order. Sub-cultures are often very active elements, deliberately negotiating and restructuring this intermediate social position. Our experience suggests that, perhaps unlike family, church and neighbourhood sub-cultures, leisure sub-cultures are an aspect of society's internal social organization which is actually thriving and constitutes a crucial vehicle through which dominant values are transmitted, resisted or negotiated and new sets of values, which may take as their point of origin a different mode of production and social organization, emerge. In particular, collective leisure offers opportunities rare – if not unique – in our society to reassert values related not to passive consumerism but to production for one's own use and enjoyment.

In this chapter we shall outline some of the defining characteristics of leisure sub-cultures. Then we shall consider in more depth the tension between the self-organized base of such sub-cultures and their professional and commercial superstructure and how this impacts upon sub-cultural attitudes towards competition and professionalism (which are both often seen to be expressions of elitist or consumerist values). The ability of a sub-culture to work through such tensions will, we hope, be shown to be considerable.

First, we must turn to examine some of the distinguishing characteristics of leisure sub-cultures.

The productive base of leisure sub-cultures

In Chapter 3 we draw attention to the important difference between leisure essentially as a form of consumption (for example, watching a cricket match, going to a drinking club, etc.) and leisure as production. Generally speaking, when leisure is enjoyed as a form of consumption it offers few opportunities for self-organization. There are some exceptions – music appreciation societies, football supporters' clubs – but as a rule it is only when people engage in leisure as active producers that they tend to combine together to form clubs and associations which are the bedrock of wider leisure sub-cultures. The extent to which individuals engage with their enthusiasm as producers or as consumers varies according to the activity. For example, the great majority of wrestling enthusiasts follow their sport as consumers. Football appears to be in decline as a spectator sport, but its amateur base seems secure. Athletics, on the other hand, is only now emerging as a spectator activity. Most crafts and hobbies are forms of 'leisure as production'. It is true that shows and exhibitions will often emerge out of such activities, but typically the visitors to such shows will themselves be enthusiasts. Finally there are some activities – sub-aqua diving and pigeon racing, for example –

which provide no opportunities for spectators whatsoever.

The relative dominance of the two forms of engagement is subject to change over time. For example, darts, snooker and even bowls have all recently provided opportunities for large-scale consumer engagement. Such sudden shifts in the primary mode of individual involvement are likely to have important effects upon the sub-culture itself.

Whilst consumer forms of engagement in leisure overlap considerably with 'spectatorism' they do not do so exclusively. Art and music appreciation societies (for example, Friends of the Bournemouth Symphony Orchestra) are forms of leisure behaviour in which individuals assume an essentially receptive or consumptive orientation without in any sense becoming 'mere spectators'. Any adequate critique of leisure as consumption must accept the validity of the 'receptive attitude'. Clearly human powers are greatly enhanced through action, doing and productiveness, but we may be guilty of a subtle form of 'masculinism' if in our eagerness to criticize leisure as consumption we dismiss as valueless all forms of passivity, quietism and receptivity. Again our experience suggests that many groups understand these arguments and have learned to value differing levels and styles of participation.

Sub-cultural homogeneity

While it is self-evident that any sub-culture must contain within itself many levels of common ideas, practices and values, it is by no means true to suggest that there is no internal differentiation or that the aspects which are common and those which are differentiated are the same for all sub-cultures. At the level of substantive activity, some sub-cultures are so highly differentiated that one wonders whether a superordinate culture can be said to exist at all. Within gardening, for example, organizations promoting specialist pursuits such as fuchsias, roses, geraniums, rhododendrons, aquatic plants, alpines and so forth, often have a more highly structured organization than generic forms of gardening themselves. Within military modelling there are significant divides – modellers, equipment modellers and diorama modellers, and now, in photography, recent changes in the technology and availability of video are leading to calls for new organizations. Within other sub-cultures the differentiation does not threaten the coherence of the total culture. Railway modelling, for example, is a very coherent sub-cultural formation, yet within it a wide variety of specialist clubs and associations exist (for example, The 2 Mil Society, with its own newsletter).

Looking at aspects of organizational structure, type and style of group, there are again many variations, from those sub-cultures such as amateur swimming where individual clubs are remarkably similar, to those in which each group runs its affairs exactly as it wishes. Thus, one may find twenty tennis clubs operating within a certain area which nevertheless exhibit totally different degrees of competitiveness and have a quite different social atmosphere, organization and so forth. Similarly we would suggest that many gardening clubs probably contain almost as many specialisms as they have members, but adopt very similar approaches to building a successful group – in other words one might find minimal variations in attitudes towards competitiveness, socializing, etc. A gardener from Leeds moving to a club in Taunton might well find herself far more at home than a footballer from north Bristol moving to a club in south Bristol. Differentiation in subject matter does not therefore have to relate to differentiation in general style or approach.

Language, rules and values

The most obvious and striking indicators of a sub-culture in operation are precisely those which we encountered immediately and described at the start of this chapter.' Particular sub-cultures will generate their own language, which may include specialist words or phrases, or perhaps just everyday words and phrases reconstructed to mean something different to the initiated individual. 'Twitchers' are over-zealous bird-watchers and are labelled as such by many conservationists, while the word 'conservationist' may be used in a derogatory manner by a member of a motor cycle scrambling club. Although the phrase 'scratch-builder' may be familiar to many model-makers (to use any found materials rather than those purpose-produced), it means something rather different to a military modeller. For them it involves the transformation of parts originally designed as something else (for example, a 'Wild West' wagon) into a military model of a very particular form (for example, a Second World War truck). Spoken language is not, however, the only form of communication. No doubt the lapidarist on holiday could recognize a fellow buff as much by what that person looks at, visits and points to as by what might be spoken. Similarly, the behaviour of people at a garden centre offers many clues as to individual specialist interests. A group of artists and a group of gardeners visiting a National Trust garden would therefore experience two entirely different places. Many activities and sub-cultures exhibit either written or informal 'rules', both for the activity and for its organization. Clearly, for most sports, the formal rules are considerable and bounded, but in many hobbies the rules are mostly unwritten. Thus, at a horticultural show, it is typical to have displays of cakes and jams – a relic of the self-sufficiency ethic of agriculture more than a hundred years ago. But, while the cakes must be home made and so must the jams, there are no formal rules for the jam used in cakes. Moreover, whilst in many large shows it is possible to submit jam made by yourself from bought fruit, at many smaller shows the fruit itself must also be self-produced.

Strong traditions, almost having the force of rules, have also emerged concerning how enthusiasts should organize themselves. The prevailing sub-culture in football has adapted some of its patterns from professional football, especially in terms of the relationship between manager, coach, team and committee (see Chapter 7). The Southfields Dynamos are subverting this tra-dition by introducing a more democratic form of organization, one which would probably be more at home in a cricket club. Within hockey, there is a tradition of having both team captains and vice-captains on the committee. Moreover, in many male sports there are clear rules about the sequence in which drinks are bought at the bar after a match.

In the following chapter we will consider the individual enthusiast and her or his needs and values and the interplay between the individual and the club. But just as the values enshrined by the club are not simply the summation of those introduced by its individual members, so the values expressed by a particular sub-culture are not reducible to those of its constituent clubs. Our impression is that different sub-cultures do express quite different values. Amateur swimming appears to be intensely competitive with a high degree of parental involvement, whereas these characteristics appear to be absent in youth football. Some sub-cultures lay great emphasis on their organization – such as photography – while for others this is a tedious practicality. Some sub-cultures take overt account of their social dimension – as with the perceived link between morris dancing and drinking – but others regard such aspects as something quite secondary which must take care of itself. In all cases, however, individual clubs bend to adapt to prevailing approaches quite considerably.

We can also add that sub-cultural variations along the lines we have described are likely to relate in some manner to other factors such as gender, race, class and perhaps age. We suggested in Chapter 3 that women may lean more strongly towards non-competitive groups and men from ethnic minorities might do the opposite. However, our sample numbers are too small to allow any definite conclusions.

The final point we wish to make is that few sub-cultures are static and many are already changing to accommodate new perspectives – for example, the approaches of women's photography groups, the widening availability of squash or golf, or the very recent interest in multi-cultural dimensions to conservation.

Institutional expression

As our cameo of the Charnwood Aquarists shows, many of the members also participate as individuals in nationally based associations with a more specialized focus. Moreover, the club itself is affiliated to the Federation of British Aquarist Societies through which it obtains judges or speakers for meetings, information on open shows, newsletters, guidance for members who wish to become judges (and hence develop an interest beyond just the club) and other services (for example, travel assistance). All of this supporting activity is not carried out by a commercial organization but by the enthusiasts themselves.

Naturally, the more popular the activity, the greater the amount of organization necessary over and above what each club can provide itself. The Leicester Premier Football League has seven divisions with fourteen teams in each. The league (rather than the city council) allocates the parks pitches to the various teams, liaises with the Parks Department over the condition of the pitches during inclement weather, allocates referees to matches, attempts to aid clubs experiencing any organizational crisis, produces a regular, quality newsletter, etc. The league itself has an organizing committee of ten people, mostly ex-players, managers or referees.

The vast majority of groups we encountered were part of some local, regional, national, even international league, federation or association. The Conwood Naturalists were not (no doubt a reflection of their self-perceived 'dabbler' status) and neither were the morris men (because they used a woman musician).

Means of communication

Each sub-culture will possess its own recognized calendar of events – shows, exhibitions, competitions, conferences, etc. Such events have complex meanings and purposes – part ritual, part solidarizing, part competitive. They are, however, an essential element in the life of the sub-culture. Our sketch of the aquarists illustrates how the club had initiated an annual show. Within most sub-cultures such shows quickly acquire a reputation for being more or less prestigious than others. The annual show at Bellevue, Manchester, is regarded as the Crufts of the aquarist world whereas for railway modellers the annual York show has the same reputation. The National Fancy Rat Society has only been in existence since 1976 and hence no particular venue has established a premier reputation. Nevertheless, a society with a total membership of just over 350 will probably run at least twenty-seven shows in one year, from Leeds in the north to Lancing in the south, and reputations and status will soon emerge.

Perhaps the most important form of communication within leisure sub-cultures occurs through the circulation of specialist magazines. Some of these (for example, *Amateur Photographer*) have an enormous circulation and are highly commercial; many, however, have tiny circulations and are produced by small groups of enthusiasts (for example, *Loco Modeller*) or by the relevant national parent institution (for example *Pro Rata*, the house journal of the national Fancy Rat Society). A visit to the local newsagent would quickly convince any sceptical reader of the sheer range of enthusiasms which now find expression in mass circulation magazines. In one local shop we counted over twenty such publications ranging from *Miniature Wargames: The Monthly Magazine for the Discerning Wargamer* to *Hobby Electronics*. Yet while shops only show a tiny fraction of available publications, those they sell relate mainly to those activities in which there is a major (perhaps majority) involvement by individual activists rather than groups. One can find, for example, at least eight publications catering for the model railway enthusiast. A glance at these would also illustrate the ability of sub-cultures to retain their autonomy, because, again, if substantive activity were the only reason for existence, then so many publications could not survive. They are able to survive because they all emphasize one particular set of sub-cultural specializations of values or another, yet often contain identical advertisements! The existence of such magazines also adds further reinforcement of each sub-culture's language, rules and values.

Closed or open systems

We have already hinted at ways in which changes in commercial or professionalized leisure can work through to sub-cultures. Boundaries to sub-cultures are therefore permeable, but this is true to varying degrees of different sub-cultures. Some we would call 'closed' systems because they express a much higher degree of autonomy from the wider social order than more 'open' systems. These terms also suggest the source of existing or new sub-cultural developments (whether they be internally or externally generated) and aspects of the direction in which change, once introduced, influences the system (either from the top down or the bottom up). The terms closed and open are therefore not implying a fixed system; they describe the mode and direction in which change occurs. Thus a very closed system will tend to generate itself internally and is most open (if at all) to pressure from the bottom up. However, even open systems can generate change from within and are not necessarily totally open to commercial and professional influence.

In railway modelling, for example, there is a long-established and consistent pattern whereby enthusiasts begin to develop a talent for a particular aspect of the activity, start to develop workshop facilities within their own home to supply local contacts, move into mail-order forms of supply and may eventually become small manufacturers with their own industrial premises. In other words, much of the manufacturing sector is internally generated. Of course there are the large firms such as Hornby, etc., but it is important to realize that these are only peripherally involved with railway modelling. (As with other forms of modelling the distinction between 'toys' and 'modelling' is essential.) There are, however, one or two large manufacturers such as PECO (a major manufacturer of '00 gauge' equipment) and Graham Parrish (of 'N gauge'). Moreover, the main magazine for enthusiasts (*Railway Modelling*) is produced by a subsidiary of PECO. Clearly a more serious investigation of this particular sub-culture would need to examine the origins of the larger manufacturing companies, their links with the enthusiasts, their marketing and product design strategies and so on. It nevertheless remains true that most of the manufacturing sector remains small-scale and is largely internally generated. It is this generation of change and initiative from the bottom up in very major ways which enables the railway modelling sub-culture to remain a fairly closed system despite the existence of apparently major private sector influence.

The contrast between this and the extremely diffuse boundaries of many sports sub-cultures could not be greater. Here the manu-facturing, the leisure media, etc., will be provided by companies which have few, if any, internal connections with the sub-culture itself. Many of the manufacturers will be subsidiary components of multinationals (for example, Dunlop). These subsidiary companies will very often possess vast product ranges, only one specialist segment of which may provide the bulk of the means of leisure production for a given sub-culture. Changes in product design may have a profound impact upon a given sub-culture and yet very often such changes may owe far more to the manufacturers competing to maintain or enhance their market share than to the needs of the enthusiasts themselves.

This is very apparent with such innovations as the large tennis racket or the dimpleless golf ball which were introduced in professional sport and were therefore external to the sub-culture. However, whilst it is not inevitable that innovations in professional activity will pass immediately down the system from the 'top', many have in fact done so, despite apparent inappropriateness. A good example, because it is about rules rather than commercial products, is the introduction of the tie-break into club tennis. This idea, the product of problems with the time management of professional tournaments, has been introduced by many clubs and leagues despite the fact that their timings and social context make its original rationale entirely irrelevant. We suspect that this may be a pattern for sub-cultures with a strong professional band; ideas come from the top down and are primarily externally generated.

Paradoxically, mountaineering resembles a closed system in terms of its institutional framework, means of communication and manner of training provision, yet most of the equipment is produced by manufacturers who are quite external to the sub-culture itself. This has led to some interesting tensions which have found expression in the correspondence columns of *Climber and Rambler* (house journal of the British Mountaineering Council). A major debate has emerged about how one evaluates 'a good climb'. Many enthusiasts feel that the modern mountaineer can make use of so many technological aids that the activity is in danger of being demeaned. Many are also becoming chary of the constant changes in fashion regarding mountaineering boots and so on. Here, then, we see a sub-culture fighting back through the reassertion of its original values in the face of commercial pressure.

The outcome of this evolving debate is not yet known, but it raises an important question about how sub-cultures can resist the types of pressure which come from both commercial and professionalized activity. While we feel that many current sub-cultures are quite solid and can reasonably be described as autonomous, potential changes may cause damage. In particular, the example from mountaineering raises the issue of the relationship between demand and supply in the production of leisure goods. Our feeling is that the more the manufacturing sector is external to its corresponding leisure sub-culture, the more likely is demand to be led by supply, whereas internally generated manufacturing is more likely to be demand-led. The marketing strategies of the leisure goods manufacturers require serious investigation, for, if it could be established that the provision of leisure goods is becoming increasingly supply-led, then a major potential threat to the autonomy of leisure sub-cultures could be established. Howard Becker's comments on photography could equally well be applied to virtually any of the forms of productive leisure we have encountered. 'Conventions specifying what a good photograph should look like are embodied not only in an aesthetic more or less accepted in the world of art photography . . . but also in the acceptance of constraints built into the neatly interwoven complex of standardized equipment and materials made by major manufacturers.'[2]

In seeking any pattern to the distribution of open, closed, internally generated, externally generated, top-down or bottom-up systems in the sub-cultures we experienced, we can return briefly to the social class issue raised earlier, and perhaps to gender and race. It is our impression that certain activities offer an opportunity for their participants to be members of sub-cultures which are more or less open. We suspect that one major attraction of certain hobbies for the working class (and perhaps for women) is that they offer a greater opportunity to share in a sub-culture which is more autonomous of prevailing commercial, professional, middle-class, masculine, competitive values than involvement in sports or certain arts. Indeed, besides the strong sense of a separate identity which many groups enjoyed, there was often a feeling of quite assertive independence. We therefore suggest that some varieties of sub-culture can be seen as a kind of counter-culture.

The 'negotiated' nature of leisure sub-cultures

We have looked at the existence of somewhat overlooked, self-organized sub-cultures and considered their variety, complexity and sometimes eccentricity. Later on we will discuss more fully the links between leisure sub-cultures and a broader concept of 'national culture' and will argue that productive engagements with leisure are in reality everyday forms of cultural production, constituting the bedrock of our culture. We continue to be astonished at the elitism of a society which tends to equate culture with the refined products of a few (for whom culture is the means to a living) and which ignores the creative activities of the vast majority of ordinary people by using the demeaning term 'leisure'.

We have suggested that sub-cultures deal almost consciously with such imposed schisms through their assertive independence. They negotiate their continued existence and development in the face of pressure from the commercial sector, commodified culture, even the rising tide of leisure professionalism in the public sector. On the one hand, one can see the universe of the formal economy, the market mass media, of professionalism in sports and elitism and c...- modification in art. On the other hand, there is the world portrayed in Chapter 3 – the world of the informal economy, of everyday, non-market forms of exchange, of self-organization and mutual aid. The values embedded within the latter universe, which Gorz[3] describes as the world of 'autonomous production', are radically different from those embedded within the formal economy; they are values of reciprocity and interdependence as opposed to self-interest, collectivism as opposed to individualism, the importance of loyalty and a sense of 'identity' or 'belonging' as opposed to the principle of forming ties on the basis of calculation, monetary or otherwise. It is these processes of negotiation that we address in the final part of this chapter by dealing more fully with issues concerning competition and professionalism, which are both thought to be signs of the inability of communal leisure to find its own autonomy within our society.

The nature of competition

Our investigation of clubs, associations and their sub-cultures revealed very clearly to us the central importance of judgement and comparison in nearly all forms of communal leisure. Almost all activities consistently offer enthusiasts opportunities to develop a sense of value and identity through their performance on the court, pool or stage, through their creations, constructions, collections or simply through their involvement in discussion and debate. However, this is not to imply that all leisure sub-cultures, individuals or groups base their existence on contest, competition and adapted professional values. There are many sports (for example, pot-holing), arts (for example, square-dancing), hobbies (for example, stamp-collecting) and crafts (for example, lapidarism) where formal competition is infrequent or non-existent, but even in these instances the process of making judgements and comparisons continues, using informal means.

We are not convinced that such processes, even when they assume an explicitly competitive form, must inevitably demean the purity of the enthusiasm itself. Our research suggests that the primary purpose of such processes is to enable individuals and groups to 'place' themselves in relationship to other enthusiasts, other groups or the sub-culture as a whole. It may be objected that the mere fact that competition and contest is the medium through which such judgements are made is sufficient to demonstrate the saturation of communal leisure with capitalist values. We would reiterate the importance of separating the institutional from the cultural frame of reference. We noted that very often, even when the activity – for example, hockey – is basically structured around competition, the dominant ethic may not be a competitive one. In other words, competitive structures do not imply competitive values. The following extracts from an interview with the manager of an amateur football club in Leicester should make the point:

> You've got two types of player – the good club man on the one hand and then, if you get a lot of success with a club, a lot of people want to join but they're pot-hunters. They perhaps come a couple of seasons, win a couple of medals and they'll be off again . . . You've got to be wise enough to say 'No, you're not coming here, not unless you're going to stop a long while and help the club out; you've got to be a good club man.

Commenting on players who leave the club for Senior league football, the same respondent said: 'A few matches later they've come back . . . they've no friends there and it's so competitive; so they come back to the club where they're enjoying it.'

These two extracts sum up neatly the tension between the dominant, competitive values common of wider society and the often suppressed values of the informal economy. The phrase 'pot-hunter' – someone whose sole imperative is to win trophies – appears to be used almost universally within different sub-cultures as a form of abuse ('trophy-hunter' is another and so perhaps is 'twitcher'). We have encountered such usage (or variations) in horticultural judging, hockey, aquarism, photography, military modelling and so forth. The phrase 'the good club man', on the other hand, illustrates the value attached to loyalty and to the notion of the club as a valued social organization in its own right rather than merely a means to personal competitive ends. Indeed, several respondents even used the metaphor of 'the family' to describe the nature of their attachment to their group.

Whilst such a tension between competitive and non-competitive values can be discerned within most leisure sub-cultures, it is also true that competitive values are stronger in some activities/sub-cultures than in other apparently quite similar ones: they are strong in amateur swimming, weak in junior football; strong in military modelling, weak in railway modelling and so forth. In particular we suspect that competitiveness is more dominant in open sub-cultures (archetypally in sports) and far less so in very closed systems such as caged-bird fancying. It also appears that women appear more likely to associate themselves with more closed and non-competitive sub-cultures, while ethnic groups either reassert their own cultural activities or, as with many Asian football teams, participate in white sub-cultures in a fiercely competitive manner in order to 'place' themselves in a hostile, white, male community.

Responding to professionalism

These dimensions also interact in complex ways with a further dimension which we have already mentioned – namely, the impact of a professional stream within any activity. In particular we have suggested that the existence of a top stratum can lead to the filtering down of values, rules and techniques but that this is not inevitable and some sub-cultures are well able to resist this tendency. Football, through the distinction between Senior and Junior activity, is an excellent example of a sub-culture negotiating the conflicts between competitiveness, the existence of a strong professional stream, a clear working-class base and a history (no less socially significant for the fact that few can take advantage) of offering working-class youth a 'way through' to another socio-economic level.[4]

Other examples offer very different solutions. Tennis, for example, has remained primarily middle-class and the sub-culture seems quite willing to accept the heavy filtering down of standards and values from its upper professional echelons, even when the innovations are clearly inapplicable lower down the system. At the opposite extreme one can find many hobbies which resolve the tensions by remaining as closed systems with few, if any, professionals. Amateur gardening resolves such tensions by invoking a set of values which distinguish it so clearly from the profession of landscape gardening that 'amateurs' actually consider the latter to be part of a totally different universe. A similar solution is used in the world of the arts – painting in particular. Here one finds different sets of values at play between the 'high' art of professional artists, galleries, critics and their attendant social circle, and the 'traditional' art which one sees in most amateur groups – representational, colourful, easy to understand rather than deliberately obscure. Almost no 'filtering down' of influence can occur, because these are indeed separate worlds, yet many members of amateur art groups adopt many of the styles and values of the art world as a whole and assert their status as 'artists'.

Comparison and judgement

The issue of standards and values also leads us to issues of judgement, to the ways in which different sub-cultures make assessments about the relative merits of enthusiasts' products or performances. The following example illustrates how a relatively closed sub-cultural system – horticulture – is able to make such judgements whilst avoiding a simple acceptance of standards imposed 'from above'.

The Leicestershire Horticultural Judges' Guild was founded in 1956 by a group of keen gardeners who were anxious to develop a network of people who could act as competent judges at flower and vegetable shows. In many other counties, gardeners from 'the big house down the road', or from the Parks Department, perform this function; in Leicestershire, however, the amateur gardeners train their own judges over a period of three years. The following are extracts taken from an interview with the president and secretary of the guild. When asked what guided them in making judgements about good quality exhibits, we were told: 'We work to the Royal Horticultural Society handbook and they give you rules for judging; that's our "bible". A lot of these Parks Department people may have looked at the RHS handbook, but they haven't learned it like we have. We've got members who can quote it *ad lib.*'

The main criteria that the RHS provide concern size, quality and condition. If this appears to be classic top-down imposition, it soon became clear that the RHS guidelines could not always be applied: 'Particularly with regard to onions, we go for the big onions. But in the mining areas of Leicestershire and Nottinghamshire they take the outer skins off and they show the onion raw. This side of the county it's against our principles, you're not supposed to do that, but this is where you have to bow to local things. Over in the mining areas, in Coalville and beyond, they'll strip the onion until you could put it in two rounds of bread. At Nottingham they have very big onions, but we've seen them took off until they've left about a quarter-inch stub at the bottom. They're taking off the damaged skin. You see, to them if the skin splits it's detrimental.'

For the local mining community, size counts for little when compared with the purity of the skin. The key point, however, is the way in which different sources of meaning and value become generated within the same sub-culture *and* such localized changes are readily accepted and respected by what could otherwise be an externally generated judging system. It is not that standards are lowered, but that sets of different criteria are introduced on top of those established formally. These less formal criteria and the processes by which they emerge are far more crucial than the formal systems, in just the same way that social dimensions to a group's existence are often more significant than its ostensible prime purpose.

It is often through such informal mechanisms such as word of mouth, rumour, casual conversation and chance encounter that reputation and status come to be bestowed on a particular type of product or a particularly 'good' enthusiast. In amateur photography, for example, we have talked to acknowledged experts who may not have exhibited competitively (indeed may not have exhibited at all) for many years. They nevertheless retain their prestige and status within the sub-culture through the wider contribution they make to any group when they visit to judge an exhibition. They may give out prizes, but their comments, their hints about forthcoming exhibitions, new techniques, difficulties at certain clubs, etc., are all valued, if anything, more than the simple judging.

A similar process can be seen at work in railway modelling. The annual Bristol Model Railway Exhibition houses upwards of twenty layouts, over thirty commercial stalls and, in the centre of the main hall, a stand at which most of the eminent 'scratch-builders' can be seen at work. These men (and they are all men) assemble model locomotives, rolling stock, etc., from scratch, using their own materials and the original specifications of the engine being modelled. One can almost feel the kind of hushed reverence which surrounds their stand as they work, using watchmakers' glasses and instruments, yet few of them have acquired their reputation through competition, as this is strongly underplayed within the sub-culture. Equally, almost all of those watching will have one or more personal favourites within the group, largely reflecting their own, or their group's, predeliction within the wide sphere of railway modelling. Nobody will be considered the 'best'.

Nevertheless, whilst such examples illustrate remarkable complexity and cultural variation, we must recognize that many activities operate quite clear, unambiguous and vigorously applied 'rules' for assessing performance. In many sports such as volleyball there is little difficulty or ambiguity in evaluating the performance of competing teams, because a points system exists which is never challenged. Thus one uses a referee rather than a judge. In other sports, however – for example, diving or gymnastics – the quality of performance is not amenable to quantitative measures, hence a need for judgement. Some sports are currently exploring the borderlines between different styles and values of judgement. For instance, take the uncertainty of a television commentator when faced with Torvill and Dean's ice-dancing. Was it sport, art or entertainment? he asked.

The degree of evaluative ambiguity is probably at its greatest in many hobbies. How does one judge the comportment of an aquarist's catfish or differentiate usefully between two pieces of weaving? Consider the dilemma faced by our colleague from the Horticultural Judges' Guild when faced with implementing rules on beetroot when 'All around the country the colours when you cut a beetroot vary according to the soil. At one show where they've got gardeners at one end of the village and gardeners at the other, there are two totally different colours.'

In such a situation precise rules often exist which purport to do away with such ambiguity, but at what cost? We support judges wholeheartedly in their mediation between national systems and local, group or even individual preferences and circumstances. If it were always the biggest cichlid that won at table shows, there is little doubt that much of the excitement which surrounds the judges' progress (and retinue) would evaporate and many aquarists would lose interest in their activity. Judges are therefore part scientist and part shaman and the show is partly clinical, partly magical and ritualistic. Rather than ranking everybody in the land (like the computer ranking of the world's professional tennis players), the whole dynamic of the sub-culture has an opposite ethos – to value everybody and permit and encourage their contribution, but without reduction to the lowest common denominator.

The examples of judging just given show quite clearly the predominance of wider social values and meanings over simplistic, functional notions of activities. Through leisure, and the existence of strong and dynamic sub-cultures, people are able to recreate a form of society and sociability lacking in industrial capitalism.

Chapter 5

The contribution of individuals to groups

In discussing the importance of sub-cultures and suggesting some ways in which they might vary between activities, there is a danger of implying that any group within a particular sub-culture is somehow a mere 'clone' pressed from a standard sub-cultural template. In relation to brass bands, for example, this would imply that all bands approach their tasks with the same degree of seriousness, with similar attitudes to the formality or informality of dress, with a bound set of acceptable pieces of music from which to select and with agreement on the relative importance of rehearsals *vis-à-vis* performances.

This is, however, very far from the truth and we can only stress the dynamic interaction between different factors which leads to the varied identities of the many groups. In this sense the relationship between groups in any sub-culture is akin to a 'confederacy' in which the general patterns remain, while the nature of each group can shape, extend, complement or reject the common patterns in what may appear to be quite dramatic ways. Thus the Southfields Dynamos, by their emphasis on a local link at the possible expense of trophies and by their extended 'democratic' structure, are stretching the conventional value-systems of the footballing sub-culture. Similarly the Matthews Morris Men, through their selection of a woman musician, are running a tightrope along the edge of the territory defined quite carefully by the Morris Ring. Even the Conwood Naturalists, in their apparent unwillingness to espouse the evangelical thrust of 1980s conservationism, are running close to the boundaries of the naturalism sub-culture.

It is not enough, however, to suggest that the final identity of any group is the result of interplay between that group and its general sub-culture. We must be able to describe the forces behind the groups which lead them to elaborate the general sub-cultural framework and to produce endless variation between individual groups. Some of these forces emerge from the environment in which a group is located (see Chapter 6), but the major shaping emerges from the interplay of the different contributions which individual members perhaps unconsciously bring to any group. It appears to us that, for most people, the elements we shall be describing form part of a semiconscious, 'mundane' or 'assumptive'[1] world in which certain aspects may be considered fairly consciously, while others remain – or are even deliberately kept – below the surface. For example, 'getting fit' may be discussed openly, while 'escaping the home' may be either acknowledged to oneself privately, or not even consciously admitted. We will cover these aspects more fully, but in general we would suggest that people bring the following elements to the groups they join:

- personal values, motivations, aspirations and needs, nearly always related to other areas of their lives;
- resources such as skills, abilities, experience, even money or access to other social/substantive networks.

One reason why people do not always openly acknowledge some of their aspirations is because of a clear recognition that membership of any group will usually demand a trading and reshaping of some values to accord with the general ethos of the group one is joining. This two-way trading can be thought of as *assimilation* – adjusting the world outside to fit your own ideas – and *accommodation*[2] – adjusting yourself to the world. Naturally this applies both to any group and to the individual member. Thus the person wishing to 'get fit' might find that a basketball club is in fact more of a fun club which runs no formal training. Three things might then occur: the group may see this new, keen player as their chance to become a little more competitive and will introduce training; the new member may become more attuned to the sheer enjoyment of playing and value the fitness less over time; or that individual may find another outlet for that objective.

Naturally there are dangers both for group and individual of being over-assimilatory or over-accommodatory. The group which refuses to adjust may find itself stranded without members while the group which is constantly readjusting may find itself with no sense of identity as a group. While the clear aim is some form of equilibrium, we located many examples of groups which exemplified noticeably different patterns to the chosen balance. The Charnwood Aquarists, for example, actually made quite conscious attempts to find out members' personal interests, to allow for these and even give them status through the group's organization. A new member with a specialized interest might well find himself or herself 'over-accepted' – by being asked to give a talk or exhibit immediately. By contrast the Leicester Penguins Swimming Club is quite clearly assimilatory in that it lays down very clear 'rules' for the involvement of any new member – not just taking part in training, but actually defining a training programme, establishing involvement either in competition or in helping with events and so forth. The new member accepts such terms or does not join.

Finally, it should also be remembered that there is in fact a three-way relationship at play. A new member may arrive at the aquarists' club as a specialist in some topic already covered by one or two other members. Even though the new 'input' may be entirely consistent with the sub-culture of the group and should be welcomed, that new member also has to negotiate with those others already specializing in that particular topic. The new competitive swimmer, keen on training, may displace another who had previously swum that particular distance and stroke. In both cases, the balance has to be sought with other individuals as well as with the general ethos of the group.

By concentrating on the process of settling into a group, we have raised two key items which require elaboration. The first point is that for many people their aspirations may, for various reasons, not be translated immediately – or even ever – into joining a group. They may lie dormant or be expressed through other forms of leisure. Secondly, even once someone has joined a group, there are important stages through which both the individual and the group as a whole must pass. Our chosen way of presenting such issues is through a simple and sequential process from the first stirrings of interest to much later adaptation to changes once one has become a group member.[4]

The impetus to join a group

Most people form value systems about the relevance to themselves of leisure in general and certain activities in particular. Our specific concern here is with the sets of values which relate to potential involvement in leisure groups rather than individual activity. In Chapter 3 we examined some of the reasons why people come together in groups. We will return to this later, but at this point we will discuss some crucial values that individuals bring to groups.

Competition

This can vary dramatically from those for whom competition is indispensable to those who resist it totally. Either set of values will automatically generate suitable lists of activities, especially because, for many, sport is associated inextricably with competition. Nevertheless, we spoke to some whose requirement for physical recreation and caution about competitiveness was served by the surprising number of clubs in which successful results were of minor importance. Another example is the growth of 'splash groups' in swimming, largely for those too old for tough competition (namely, over twenty), but who still wish to meet together for pool-based activity.

Recreation

This refers to notions of 'escape', of 'doing something different', meeting new people, avoiding work or even home. Again there are extremes, from those who indulge in recreation in what to them is a totally non-work manner, to those who consider that, to recreate properly, one must 'work hard at it'. There are also extremes from those whose selection reflects a wish to avoid any link with work/home and those – typically many naturalists and sport teachers – for whom their group activity is deliberately a 'busman's holiday'. Both sets of values are about the separation of recreation from 'life' or its reciprocation if it.

Sociability

While the sociableness of a group may rarely be offered as a prime reason for joining, there can be little doubt that a group's social atmosphere figures very highly for some of its members. Nearly all groups we encountered had some kind of formal social life, often linked to fund-raising. As our cameo of the Conwood Hockey Club illustrates, the value of the group's social side varies for different members and such variations can be a source of tension. We must, however, make clear a distinction between the sociableness of a group and its social nature. The social nature of communal leisure groups resides in their common character as a site for the generation and reinforcement of sub-cultural elements and also, among other things, of ritual, solidarity and identity. Moreover, while all groups are social, they are not all sociable.

Standard

We have already examined the difference between a wish to 'place' oneself and a wish to be competitive. Most people will make personal judgements about the level at which they are satisfied with their contribution to a group. This may not equate with that group's judgement of worth. Thus a middle-aged hockey player may consider 'retiring' because of failing ability long before her group become dissatisfied with her contribution. Alternatively, a painter may be quite willing to stay with a group (if the group is sufficiently accommodating) even if his ability remains patently below that of any other member. It is particularly in relation to personal standards –

dramatically in sport – that one sees changes as one gets older (although a growing unconcern for competitiveness may mean a wish to continue for sheer personal enjoyment).

Involvement

It is commonplace to divide our world into 'joiners and non-joiners'. In terms of involvement one might reconstrue this as 'organizers and never-organizers'. A fairly common comment received during our research was that 'it's no good joining a group unless you are willing to work for it'. However, we also became aware of an alternative conviction – that membership of a group is for recreation not work (namely, organizing). In Chapter 6 we examine further the divisions within groups, but would warn against too easily categorizing one perspective (involvement) as 'good' and the other (passivity) as 'bad'.

Production/consumption

Even within mutual aid forms of communal leisure there are differing balances between production and consumption, each attracting different people. At one extreme (perhaps military modelling), the prevailing values may be about a narrow, even selfish, notion of production strictly for self-consumption. At the opposite extreme, the values are more akin to those of 'service for others' embedded in traditional voluntary action. Between the two one could point to many judo clubs where the club is run by adults for their own children. Individuals seeking group membership may well be predisposed to one or other of these orientations.

Rarely, however, will any sub-culture or even single group exhibit or permit only one of these orientations. Thus the Warmley Golden Hours Club displayed elements of both extremes. One of the key organizers of this club for the elderly – herself well over sixty-five – talked about her contribution to the 'old people' as if she herself was still only twenty-five! She brought with her a strong work ethic and showed clear pride in the club as her own creation. However, she would sometimes refer in a resigned fashion to certain members who came along, enjoyed (or more often complained about) the afternoon's activities but never gave anything back in return, treating the club as just one more stopping point in the weekly circuit of clubs.

Individual versus group

Activities may be preferred precisely because they do or do not offer 'team' attributes. Football cannot be pursued without teams, sculpture cannot easily be pursued by groups. Between the two one finds interesting sub-cultural variations, as with rifle shooting. Here the club may send a 'team', but each person shoots as an individual and this is reflected in the allocation of prizes. In the example we studied (the East Bristol Rifle and Pistol Club), there was some resistance to the committee's attempts to select and control coherent teams. However, we found no correlation between sociability and team games. It is often suggested that athletics is for 'loners', but we found many people who, while being very socially orientated, could not countenance working in a group or playing team games.

We must also consider the factors which motivate people towards action. We would argue that involvement in leisure, specifically in groups, offers the individual an opportunity to find a role which is an escape from, a partnership with or a reinforcement of that person's role at home, at work or even in other leisure or social settings. Such motivations are not a simple one-to-one response to home or work circumstances, but will change as these circumstances change over time. Consider Kathy, who was, at the time of our contact, producer for the Oldville Players. After moving to Oldville and having children, she felt unable to pursue her acting career with the Kelvin Players (a major Bristol amateur group). The Oldville Players were clearly below her standard but, at that time, that was exactly what she wanted. At the Kelvin Players, however, she had always only acted and yet harboured thoughts of one day doing some production work. Her new-found role as producer in Oldville was therefore highly appropriate both to her and to the local players, to whom a quality actress could have been a slight embarrassment.

Some of the clearer motivations are easy to describe. In terms of escape from work, the example we have already given on onion growing in mining communities provides one illustration. We could cite other working-class examples of leisure escapism such as breeding pigeons, cultivating flowers, even 'rambling'. A different example comes from one of our colleagues at work. He is very involved in management courses at the School for Advanced Urban Studies and yet has steadfastly succeeded in keeping this fact from others in his sailing club. He realizes that this knowledge could lead to pressures on him to participate in the running of the club – a role he is explicitly attempting to avoid through that activity. Perhaps the archetypal example of escape from home is the housewife. We met a number of women who made it clear to us that their involvement in a group was, if anything, directed more towards avoiding the home than towards the selected activity or group. For some of these women the objective of meeting people – 'company' – was stated explicitly and their 'selection' of a group occasionally involved little more than tagging along with a friend.

In terms of reinforcement of work, the most common example is that of the person who deals with figures and money at work who then takes on (or is persuaded into taking on) such a role in the group, as treasurer. The archetype here may be the accountant, but the treasurer (later chairman) of Oldville Players is an administrator of a further education college, the treasurer of Southfields Dynamos had worked as an accounts clerk and the treasurer of Monktonians Football Club was a ledger clerk. Apart from occasional ventures on to the pitch by the Dynamos' treasurer, none of these three are participants in the main group activity – the first has never acted, the last has never played football! A less common but distinctive example is that of the secretary of the Downend Cricket Club who consciously sought a management role in his club in order to bring to it the skills he could not always use as a senior manager in Rolls-Royce, though he was very aware of the dangers of direct transfer of models: 'If you happen to have got some experience of management, it's interesting to try it. It's certainly a very different world from being in an industrial setting. It poses problems that you don't think about in your normal life. When you're dealing with people, you're always learning.'

Examples of the reinforcement of one's home role are less common except at an almost stereotypical level. We lost count of the number of wives who saw their major contribution to their group (or often their husbands' group) to be 'making the teas' or the drama costumes. For men, do-it-yourself skills were commonly brought to bear.

Finally, in relation to links with an individual's other leisure or social activities, we suspect that we located more of a consensus than a variety. Rather than finding people who were heavily involved with one club deliberately choosing to take a more passive role in their other social/leisure relationships, we found that organizers in one club were probably also organizers in at least one other. Social secretaries were often well-known local organizers of social events and probably well known amongst their neighbours in the street.

Finding an outlet

We have already suggested that many values and motivations remain either unfocused or even deliberately submerged. There are several reasons for this, which often hinder the direct translation from aspirations into actions.

Some motivations may be socially illegitimate to admit openly, even to oneself. Thus, our society tends to be most concerned with functional reasons for joining a group. Someone will join a numismatic society because of an interest in collecting coins. Social reasons for joining (for example, escape from household drudgery) tend to be devalued and cannot comfortably be presented as a basis for commitment to a club.

By devaluing or pushing aside such motivations, we suspect that losses sometimes occurred either for groups or individuals. A group might attribute its failure in attracting members to regular training sessions to a lack of keenness or competitiveness, when in fact their members lay special value on weekend rather than weekday (or workday) activity. Equally, an individual might attribute her failure in settling in to a netball club solely to a perceived decreased ability in netball (which may or may not be real) rather than to failure to tune in to the often subtle social mores of the club. In both cases the obvious 'solution' (dropping all training or leaving the club) may be an inappropriate response. We must also add that non-elaboration of motivations can lead to pleasant surprises. The netball player could find that an original search for a certain competitive standard is now, on reflection, less significant than the social contacts.

This is thus a further dimension to the 'trading' mentioned earlier. Very often an individual's motivations really only become clear after some time in a group. However, it should also be remembered that too elaborate an awareness of one's own aspirations is almost certain to lead to frustration because, except by chance, no group will offer exactly the niche one seeks. We argue that many groups prefer to maintain an ambiguity and lack of clarity in their internal conduct partly because it is this that creates the space for that mostly unspoken trading that occurs between individual members and the group. Thus, perhaps contrary to certain prevailing ideas about management in the voluntary sector, we suggest that many organizations of the mutual aid sort appear to have sound reasons for maintaining a lack of clarity about their objectives and methods. (There are, of course, some dangers to such ambiguity which we will consider in Chapter 7.)

Something as conscious as a 'search' for a group may not take place, nor is any 'choice' necessarily made except by default. What is certainly clear is that any choice which is made contains far more than a simple wish to create jewellery or play netball. Certainly there are those for whom a substantive activity is of major importance – and can outweigh negative social aspects – but we suspect that these are relatively few. The crucial point is that most publicity and advertising of groups concentrates solely on the actual activity itself rather than any other dimension. The actual selection or adoption (our preferred term) of any activity must therefore rely on other levels of discrimination. The model mentioned earlier[3] suggests a number of conditions under which adoption actually occurs and these warrant some brief discussion.

Opportunity

This includes physical access, physical abilities, availability of finances and access to resources.

Knowledge

This involves knowledge of the nature and requirements of the activities, for example, can one be a beginner, does one require equipment of one's own, do they run teams, etc; also, whether there is a club nearby. If so, one has to find out something about its social composition, whether one will be expected to take on some role, stay around for a drink afterwards, etc.

Social milieu

This includes the effects of membership on family and friends, perhaps even colleagues at work.

Receptiveness

This is primarily concerned with readiness to move into something new (or return to something). It seems likely that the final impetus is often given by some change, perhaps very minor, in personal circumstances (now the children are at school I can join that club, etc.). This is significant because it suggests a need for some event or encounter which actually transforms what may be an unfocused aspiration into action. Such key events are likely to be 'accidental' rather than connected directly with the activity.

The reader will recall the two members of the Conwood Naturalists, one who was brought along by a friend, the other whose interest in naturalism had lain dormant until retirement. Also there was the morris dancer who 'had no interest whatsoever in dancing of any sort' until his son started. He and his wife became a 'taxi service' and eventually he 'stopped a couple of nights and they roped me in. It was half voluntary. They managed to twist my arm eventually.' One couple had become involved in archery because the husband had become disabled, sought out a sport, enjoyed the activity until his wife, who was a 'taxi driver', became involved. The current secretary of the Charnwood Aquarists was originally told about the club by a carpet fitter who noticed her fish tank. A photography club contained a number of people who had tried out different activities in a series of evening classes until they found something upon which they wished to concentrate, and also some who had been stimulated by the club's annual exhibition.

We could list a remarkable range of key events and would assert that, from our experience, these were predominantly not apparently related to a conscious search for the right club. Even some who moved to a new area and deliberately sought out a squash or drama club would eventually make a selection with criteria in mind other than simple standards of performance. However, while some events are accidents, many are a quite natural outcome of local social processes and, rather than groups simply ending up with some purely fortuitous collections of people, they do – if mostly unconsciously – use social networks to attract those who will make appropriate contributions to the groups. In other words, in any social milieu, new members are often as much sought after as seeking and the criteria for a 'good group member' may be very wide indeed.

Settling in

What happens once a choice has been made? The process of settling in, or 'induction', will be examined in Chapter 7 from the point of view of the group, but the other side of this trading of values – the assimilation and accommodation we described earlier – relates to the way in which individuals adjust.

There are in fact two rather different patterns to the adjustment. The first is when an individual arrives with certain aspirations and expectations, finds that the group requires or offers a rather different balance (for example, of competitive and social values) and then has to choose either to adjust, attempt to change the group or leave. The second, however, is rather different, being those occasions on which membership of a group is discovered to offer more, different and generally better experiences than had been expected. This was reported to us very strongly by members of the Soar Valley Gardening Club who arrived as beginners and were extremely cautious about how they might be received by the experts. They also expected a series of talks by outside experts presented very much as lectures. In reality the club made newcomers very welcome, was sympathetic to the needs of such new arrivals and even arranged its evenings in such a way that the newest member felt able to ask a question without embarrassment.

We also encountered examples such as the new member of a cricket club who felt that the standard was rather low but remained because he liked the social atmosphere and the club was local. One or two of the members of Southfields Dynamos, while pleased to be involved in the committee, felt that they were actually being over-pressured into taking a role. The member of the Conwood Naturalists who joined on retirement was also the one who commented on their status as 'dabblers'. He nevertheless stayed because the Bristol Society was too 'high-powered' and too far away. A new member of the Leicester Penguins Swimming Club had apparently left after a few weeks because he had not realized how good they were and the extent to which they emphasized rigorous training and competition. Someone who had recently joined the East Bristol Rifle and Pistol Club had a similar reaction, as well as a concern about the costs of equipment. In her case, however, she stayed because the club made clear that competition was not as necessary as it had seemed and that she could build up her equipment over time with help from members.

Not surprisingly, we encountered more examples of pleasant surprises on joining a group than examples of conflict between individual and group expectations (partly because we only heard at second hand about those who left groups). The story about the swimming club came from someone who had joined with a very clear expectation about commitment and competition but who had then discovered an excellent social atmosphere as well. Members of the Matthews Morris Men commented that they had not realized the existence of annual conferences, books, magazines and links to other sub-cultures such as folk music. New arrivals at the Charnwood Aquarists, much like those at the Soar Valley Gardening Club, had been pleasantly surprised at the varied resources and opportunities offered by the group. On one occasion we met a woman who had established a personal 'rule' that she would never get involved in organization but had slowly come to realize that it need not be very onerous and also that by being involved she could better ensure that the group continued to satisfy her needs. Perhaps the most common adjustment was by those who came ostensibly in search of a competitive attitude and standard but who then stayed because this began to fade in significance in relation to other social qualities of the particular group. In essence, though, the group experienced by settled members was not the same as the one they had expected or first encountered – their own attitudes and motivations would often change as might some of the approaches of the group itself.

Finding a niche and changes over time

Settling in is, however, only a first stage. Once settled, a new member will nevertheless be distinctive and be dealt with in a special way for some period of time. During this period other members will make a point of seeing that the person is clear about what to do (for example, that *all* members contribute to the annual show) and they will also be watching for any new role which that new member seeks or for which he might be deemed appropriate. Also during this period the individual may conceal his own values if these conflict with group values or may remain reticent about other skills he has.

At some point, however, that member will cease to be regarded as 'new'. At this point certain aspirations which might have been considered too awkward at first can be given free rein – as with the secretary of a drama group who saw an opportunity to steer the group back to 'straight' drama from pantomimes. One can urge more effort and greater competitiveness without being regarded as too 'pushy' or, as in the case of the aquarist and gardening clubs, one can settle down to be an 'expert' in one's own right. In fact, these two groups were interesting in that almost every member was regarded as an expert in some aspect of the subject (or on social events, etc.) but without any explicit labelling taking place. The specific contribution each person made to the group was seen to be a natural response, not needing any formal recognition through titles and roles. By avoiding labelling, the group also offers the chance – without stigma – for someone to have no special contribution or to be involved minimally. If roles and titles are attached to individuals, this can heighten division and also mean that there is automatic pressure to 'fill' any role when someone leaves. The ability to sustain diversity and to cope with change comes not from full, vigorous and totally open exploitation of every nuance of individual and group needs (probably a myth anyway), but from the creation of action space for individuals within what is nevertheless a very clear and distinctive overall group identity. The clear identity provides the stability within which individual motivations can evolve.

The need for action space to accommodate all the variations should be clear, but the picture is complicated further by the fact that changes to the circumstances of members are regular occurrences. The major changes occur in relation to such familiar events as marriage, bereavement, birth of children, children going to school, children leaving home, retirement, physical deterioration or sudden disability, even moving house, changing job and so forth.

The St Mark's Trampoline Club in Leicester started up just over ten years ago following advice by a doctor to the husband of a woman who was dying of cancer to 'find an interest'. Two of his children were interested in trampolining, the nearest club was Birmingham, so they established one in Leicester. He had never trampolined in his life before, but is now the respected coach of a club which has acquired a national reputation. The leader of the Outlook Boys' Club had to reconsider his commitment because his new job involved overtime and travelling. One member of the Monktonians' Football Club was struggling with domestic pressures since his wife had given birth to a son, while another found conflict between his role of secretary and his role as a teacher. Within many sporting sub-cultures there appears to be a tradition whereby those who can no longer play move into club administration and then some, on retirement (and the acquisition of limitless time?), move into league administration. Also there is a tendency for husband-and-wife involvement in activity (for example, drama and archery) to become husband-only after the birth of children. Again, in many sports, the first flush of vigorous competition often gives way to a more relaxed attitude and many of the captains of lower elevens in hockey are former, older but very experienced first team players.

Perhaps the best example we can supply is that of the producer from the Oldville Players. We have already noted how her attitude to 'seriousness' had changed from her days with the Kelvin Players, following from marriage, moving and the birth of her children. Her role as producer is now a perfect reflection of her position in the group, especially as her children are now getting older; she is within the group but clearly also different. In our interview with her we asked about the future. She and her family were about to move further from Bristol and out of Oldville. While many group members stay with their old clubs (if they do not move too far), in her case the change was making her re-examine her role. With her children reaching an age at which they might be left alone, and with the family economy stretching to two cars, she had begun to think about rejoining the Kelvin Players. While our questioning had not initiated such thoughts, it was only on reflection that she herself realized the pattern of her activities over fifteen years or so.

In Chapter 7 we will consider how, for example, the Oldville Players as a group adjust to such complex, individual changing patterns.

Chapter 6

The environment of groups

In Chapter 5 we introduced the notion of equilibrium between a group and its individual members, while Chapter 4 described the sub-cultures within which groups operate. The latter are clearly a part of any group's environment, but we would argue them to be of considerable importance. Groups are also influenced by the contributions of their members, but in a description of the interplay between an 'organism' and its 'environment' no simple, uni-directional model is adequate. To use the Gestalt[1] concepts of 'figure' (our groups) and 'ground' (their environment or setting), it should be clear by now that the figures are not merely the shape left by an all-determining ground, yet neither are they rigid, unchanging and determinants of their own ground. Some level of interaction takes place and it is to this that we must return when we have completed our map of the 'ground'. Bearing in mind that individuals and sub-cultures are also part of any group's setting, we describe here five other components:

- the local community within which a group exists;
- leagues, associations, etc. (considered here from an organizational perspective rather than the cultural perspective offered in Chapter 4);
- the commercial sector covering everything from the professional aspects of sport, crafts, etc., to the provision of equipment or sponsorship;
- the public sector, including 'hardware' (pitches, etc.), 'software' (people, etc., support, grants and so forth);
- the independent sector.

The major part of the chapter will discuss each in turn. In the second competitiontakes place between the club members (and their 'intermediary' organizations, one a primarily autonomous community association, the other a public sector community college. The term 'intermediary' refers to the way in which such organizations occupy and manage a territory between the groups on the one hand and the public sector on the other – a relationship which can otherwise become difficult or inequitable for the former.

The local community

This phrase probably evokes images of a relatively small and coherent neighbourhood within which one might find, for example, a gardening club and a couple of football teams. Such clubs would draw all their members from the neighbourhood, although a few might come from further afield, usually because of some personal link such as relatives or friends.

While many of the groups we encountered were of this general type, it is very important to recognize and appreciate those other groups who do not relate simply to any single geographical area or social community. There are several quite powerful and valid reasons for the existence of such groups and their lack of a local link cannot be considered in any way a weakness.

First of all, many activities are less popular and/or more specialized. A generalized gardening club may exist in a town because there are too few fuchsia, clematis, rose, alpine and rhododendron enthusiasts to form separate clubs for each. Such specialized groups – for example, the Bristol Ornithological Society – tend to operate over a much larger geographical area, in their case the whole of Avon county. Members may belong both to that society and to their local naturalists' group. There are regional variations, but the pattern tends to demonstrate, as with the Matthews Morris Men in Leicester, a reliance upon urban centres both for reasons of accessibility and availability of materials, teachers, etc. This latter point is of increasing significance, as the Matthews Morris Men demonstrate. They meet at a point fairly central for the whole group and in a room which was available when they formed. The St Matthew's Centre is, however, also a centre of its own neighbourhood and is trying to stimulate local activity. Will groups such as Matthews Morris Men find themselves ousted in favour of highly local groups, perhaps as a result of an assumption about the relative social values of local and non-local?

Secondly, many activities with a clear 'top' strand of activists, especially sports, cannot cater for such top performers except at a city or even regional level. One reads of young swimmers travelling many miles early every day to practise, and top cricket and tennis clubs have extremely large catchment areas. In London, the London Hockey League, arguably the best in the country, is composed largely of teams whose members are drawn from anywhere in London or the home counties. But such teams are very often also part of a larger hockey club which fields several other teams of a lower standard and these teams may well have a more 'local' catchment area. At the very top levels, however, one also hears of people moving house to be near to specialist facilities, coaches and clubs.

Thirdly, some activities – for example, sea-angling for Kingswood residents or rock-climbing for those in Leicester – simply cannot be undertaken without travel to the particular location or facility necessary. This can tend to mean that groups attract members from huge catchment areas – for example, to a sailing club on a reservoir in the Peak District – but this pattern is not the only one. The Warmley Deep Sea Anglers, for example, are a very localized group of people who meet together to travel out to selected fishing spots. The difference lies perhaps in the control of the key resources – lake or beach. For the former, it is a particular lake only that matters and therefore the sailing club will be based alongside its resource. For the latter, there are very many beaches to choose from and the angling club can be based anywhere where sea angling enthusiasts are to be found.

It may be concluded that the localism of a group is a fixed characteristic. This is far from true in that, for instance, a highly local group may perform very well and slowly attract people from further afield to retain its standards. Conversely, a group which meets in a 'local' centre such as St Matthew's may slowly find (perhaps because of travel costs) that its 'outside' members are replaced by those from the local area. The provision of new facilities can also change a pattern – as when a local authority has a choice between building a leisure pool (with 'beaches' and wave machine) or a competitive pool, either of which will generate (and inhibit) certain local and non-local activities.

One key point, however, about many of these groups which are not tied to a specific locality is that they can nevertheless be a part of a very strong sub-cultural community. Other groups may also have a choice about whether to stay local and general or become more specialized. The Soar Valley Gardening Club had deliberately chosen to operate at the level of the 'family gardener' in order to involve local enthusiasts. The East Bristol Model Railway Society has no particular sense of identity with its area, despite the fact that many of its members come from north-east Bristol and work for the same employer (British Aerospace). The group does, however, have a very strong identity with its railway modelling sub-culture.

The critical academic assessments of the idea of 'community' in the 1970s[2] were made very much in relation to the cosy and often romanticized notions then current amongst planners and architects. Their critics argued that not only were the myths about community unfounded, but also that any last vestiges of communal relations bounded by physical form had been eroded by shifts in employment, social mobility, education, television and so forth.[3] Geographical identities had been replaced with 'communities of interest' and 'community without propinquity'.[4] More recently, however, it has become possible to reassert the values of community and neighbourhood – even if without recourse to idealized notions of perpetual and always benevolent social exchange.[5]

In our interviews respondents would frequently offer information about what they themselves would term their 'local community'. More specifically, they would offer some description of the character of their group and hint that such a character is inevitable 'in this area'. The Conwood Naturalists argued their very low-key approach was relevant to their neighbourhood, that the people were quite 'ordinary' and were just coming for a 'nice evening out'. The thrust for competitive standards in a judo club was presumed to reflect the very 'pushy' local parents.

There were major variations in what constituted the local area, although the more central location of the Leicester study area tended to provide our sample with a higher proportion of city-wide than local groups. Here also the social class and ethnic variations between areas tended to lay down quite strong boundaries and quite tightly localized groups. In Kingswood the situation was quite different in that the heart of many small areas was very clear, but the precise boundaries between them were unclear, even if almost all groups stated very firmly the area which they considered their group to serve. In general, though, we gained a clear impression that, for example, a Warmley group would be different from a Hanham group in the same way that Warmley is different from Hanham – even if conventional social indicators would not pick up such differences.

We must, of course, point out again that such factors as local character would be of no significance at all if membership of a group was determined solely by the standard of its activity. If that were the case, then very simple classifications and rankings would be possible and any potential participant would simply choose the nearest group to offer the relevant activities and standards. In the previous chapter we have argued that in reality individuals choose to belong to groups for a number of reasons other than the nature and standard of its activity.

Actually, we have found that many groups do develop a continuing and reciprocal relationship with their local community. We cannot offer concrete evidence, but we suspect that the intention of the Southfields Dynamos to remain locally based rather than (as they construed it) bring in better players from outside was because of a wish to reassert the character of Southfields as an area and to contribute to its regeneration. Members of the Oldville Players, in describing their decision not to participate in the *Evening Post*

Rose Bowl Competition (run by an Avon-wide newspaper), also reflected a wish to serve Oldville and its people, who form the majority of the group's audiences. They also made clear that the majority of this audience, although advertised for widely, not only came from their 'village' (their term) but were also known personally to someone or other in the group. Both of these examples, however, show reciprocity occurring in an almost unconscious fashion. Our one example of overt use of reciprocity therefore demands some attention.

The example is the Overseas Cricket Club in Leicester, established in 1974 from within the Asian community of Belgrave but now having a number of non-Asian players, whose first team use a pitch owned by a West Indian businessman. The club now runs several teams and has slowly worked its way up the ladder of local leagues (one's own pitch being essential at senior levels of competition) until it now provides occasional players for the county youth team. If, however, one were to examine the locus of the individuals' efforts within the club, one would probably find that the actual cricketing activities are outweighed by all the other social activities which they arrange, not just for their own members but for the whole of the Belgrave community. Cricket could even be considered the 'excuse' for the other activities, or even a means to clearly admitted social ends. It is perhaps only in a Hindu-dominated culture that such explicit social aims are possible; reflecting that religion's sense of a spiritual purpose to all aspects of life and its denial of a distinctive 'secular' territory.

If we are correct in our assertion that groups are not merely located within a particular community but also engaging with and contributing to that community (despite their apparently 'exclusive' membership conditions), there are some significant lessons for community development and particularly for grant aiding. We could perhaps begin to think of community development (as does the Arts and Recreation Department of Leicester City Council) in terms of leisure development.

National bodies and local leagues

In almost all the areas of activity we studied we eventually came across the existence of corresponding national or regional 'parent body' or 'umbrella body' organizations. In many competitive sports and pastimes such organizations will be nationally based and, because competition is conditional on the club's membership of such national bodies, they assert a powerful influence. The Amateur Swimming Association, for example, has a formidable rule book to which any competitive swimming club must adhere. The Football Association has branches and officers at county level as well as national level and, just as the local leagues supervise and support the activities of individual clubs, so the county FA supervises and supports the activities of the local leagues.

It is possible, of course, to find some activities where the national body is very strong (for example, the National Morris Ring), yet it is possible for clubs (for example, Matthews Morris Men) to survive outside it. In all instances so far considered, the national body is a governing body – that is, it has power to legislate and sanction. Some national bodies, the Ramblers' Association for example, assume the form of federal (or 'umbrella type') organizations rather than ones with governing powers. Here the relationship is a permissive/supportive one. There is no obligation on the club to be a part of the national body; clubs affiliate because they want to, not because they have to. At the far end of this continuum one encounters activities where not only are there no governing bodies, but there are no national 'umbrella type' bodies either. There may, however, be local and regional ones. Thus in drama the Oldville Players were aware of the existence of the Avon Federation of Drama Societies, yet had decided that membership would bring them few benefits. On the other hand, the East Bristol Model Railway Society is a member of the Wales and West of England Federation of Model Railway Societies, largely because of the role the federation performs as a collective medium through which regional exhibitions can be mounted and co-ordinated.

Here we would like to focus upon the practical contribution made by such national and regional organizations to the individual clubs and their members. We have found six distinct forms of support which are offered.

Organization

Undoubtedly the organization of a large netball league or a series of gardening shows is a major task. In smaller leagues and associations such organization may be performed simply by arranged meetings of club secretaries (for example, annually to settle a fixture list), while larger bodies require a major commitment of time beyond that achievable simply by club secretaries. This leads to the existence of an informal body of organizers not above that of individual groups nor entirely detached from them. Indeed, our experience was that many such organizers are either retired group members (no doubt with experience of organizing their club) or senior but still 'ordinary' group members. There are also many activities for which a national or regional tier of paid employees exists – the Caravan Club, the Lawn Tennis Association and so forth.

Judging

The training, registration and organization of judges, referees, umpires and so forth is one of the key functions performed by national governing bodies. In aquarism, for example, the Federation of British Aquarist Societies organizes regular weekend schools for individual club members who wish to obtain competence in judging. The federation has three categories of competence – class A, B and C – which pertain to different standards of competition. A class C judge, for example, can be invited to a club's own table show where competition takes place between the club members (and their fish!) only. Only class A and B judges, however, can attend open shows where competition takes place between aquarists throughout the region. Within aquarism the allocation of judges to shows is performed by the clubs themselves – that is, they invite the judge they prefer within the appropriate category. In many sports, however, the allocation of judges and referees to contests and games is performed by the governing body. For example, the Leicestershire and Rutland County Football Association (which has one full-time employee) oversees the allocation of its several hundred registered referees to amateur league games throughout the county. If two teams were to play without a registered referee present they would face severe disciplinary action.

Newsletters, etc.

Our concern here is primarily publications produced by local leagues and federations rather than magazines obtaining national circulation. Even so, the range of product can be considerable, from an occasional one-page, photocopied newsletter to regular, properly printed journals with illustrations and advertising. Some must be extremely expensive to produce, even allowing for any advertising revenue. To give an example, one of the two main amateur football leagues based in Leicester produces a high-quality, twelve-page quarterly newsletter. Besides the usual run-of-the-mill information on league placings, problems with pitches, etc., each newsletter contains a regular column contributed by an international standard referee and a special feature page in which each club in the league takes turns to talk about itself. Similarly, the Western Counties Photographic Federation produces a regular newsletter, alerting members to shows, exhibitions and club meetings, as well as an annual directory of clubs and judges.

Supplies

It may only be in the area of leisure that one can now find shops run by enthusiasts or practitioners. Naturally there are many occasions on which membership of a group can bring simple financial benefit, bulk purchase of photographic materials for example, but we also found that rooting some supply within a given sub-culture is regarded as some form of guarantee, even if the product being recommended is more expensive than some others. In the world of model railways or military modelling, some materials and equipment are only available through the sub-culture and membership of a group. No doubt the certainty of a market is of more value to a producer than risky diversity. Apparently many railway modelling societies in Bristol tend to 'adopt' particular model shops and then not only use such venues for purchasing, but also for informal social gatherings. Anyone trying to get served in a model shop on a Saturday morning must be aware of the 'floating' population, most of whom are not really there to buy anything!

Insurance

There are some activities – notably archery and rifle shooting – for which one cannot easily obtain licences, premises or insurance except as a member of a group. Other forms of insurance for group possessions or premises are often available at cheaper rates if one's group is involved with a league or association. Naturally, most groups with distinctive premises and possessions will be members of some league or association but some are not – for example, a small non-competitive badminton group. In some cases the group insurance can only be obtained through group membership of the appropriate association. The offer by leagues and associations of reduced rate insurance is, of course, also a way of ensuring compliance by the group with some of its basic rules.

Aid and advice

Magazines catering for particular enthusiasms can be seen as a way of offering aid and advice to what might otherwise be fiercely independent groups and individuals. The role of judges and referees can also be considered in this light. On one occasion someone who acts as a judge for regional photographic exhibitions admitted quite openly that the real purpose behind the invitations he receives to judge a club's competition lies not in the actual judging but in the subsequent question-and-answer session. He also admitted that this still makes it difficult to help a group with organizational difficulties – that remains taboo. The need for aid and advice was clear.

The commercial sector

Groups are influenced by the commercial sector in several ways. As we experience the leisure boom, it appears that the influence of this sector is increasing. The nature of its impact remains ambiguous, in part reflecting the fact that it is probably as inaccurate to describe the disparate activities of commercial organizations as a 'sector' as it is for us to use this term for the groups we have been studying. Nevertheless, we suggest four elements of private/commercial influence as follows.

Professionalism

We have commented already on the variations between arts, sports, crafts and hobbies in terms of the existence (or otherwise) of a professionalized stream and the effect which this may have on groups within each sub-culture. While it is important to remember that professional streams may have no influence at all, there are three ways in which they may do. First of all through the values central to any activity – for example, the impact of the 'professional foul' in football down through the ranks to any recreation ground kick-around, or perhaps the effects of television coverage of darts, shifting emphasis from teams to the individualization demanded by the media. The second means of influence is through rules; sporting examples are again the most obvious. We have discussed the tie-break in tennis and a similar effect has occurred with limited overs cricket. Again this was introduced at a professional level for commercial reasons and has been adopted (not without resistance) by many small clubs and leagues. Yet, as our earlier example of horticultural judging shows, many hobby sub-cultures display a firmer attitude regarding change from above, even when, as with dog-breeding, there is a clear professional stream. The third way in which professionals can influence the activity of enthusiasts is through choice of equipment. We can offer examples of the inappropriate adoption of professional practices at amateur levels. The large golfball and the extra large tennis racket are two examples of equipment needing more rather than less skill to gain any benefit, yet both are now adopted at amateur levels throughout those sports. The controversy emerging within the mountaineering community concerning its increasing dependence on technical equipment rather than climbing skill shows that change is not inevitable or uncontested. On the other hand, there are several examples showing the often liberating effect of making new technology more widely available. Perhaps the best example of this is colour printing for amateur photographers – something which used to be the preserve of professionals and the very rich but which is now available to most clubs and also to many individuals without ridiculous expense. The impact of a demanding group of consumers Cannot be overlooked here because, for example, silk-screen printing (technically far easier to make more widely available) has not yet truly moved beyond a specialist activity because of simple lack of demand.

Products

The type of equipment just described illustrated an aspect of the top-down diffusion of new products within leisure, yet equipment constitutes a small proportion of the total range of products provided by the private sector as the 'means' of leisure activity. Leisure is undoubtedly a boom business and many companies rely increasingly on this part of the market for their survival – and for any future growth. Naturally the largest part of this market is the individual consumer, even if that consumer is a member of a group. Indeed, it is unlikely that any major manufacturer does or could survive strictly through supply to groups alone. There must surely be many more individuals who paint in oils entirely alone than as members of groups; the same must be true for gardening and probably for cruiser sailing. For most sports the situation is probably the reverse: most golfers are members of clubs, as are most cricketers (at least those needing and buying the whole range of equipment). Promotion of products to such groups therefore comes most sensibly through relevant sub-cultural journals rather than through general retail outlets and advertising.

More importantly, however, there are some products which are purchased by groups alone rather than individuals – cricket rollers, goal posts, judo mats, some specialist photographic equipment, expensive manuals and guides and so forth. Apart from local authorities, schools and some private clubs, communal leisure groups must be an important market for many producers.

Premises

While it may still be true that the majority of pitches and premises for sport in Britain (as compared to the USA, for example) are provided by the public sector, the picture changes dramatically when all leisure activities are considered. As will be seen in the next chapter, a majority of groups in Kingswood use facilities which are not distinctively public. The reason for this phrase will emerge as we illustrate a number of types of provision.

Our first category we call *private clubs*. This includes many squash centres, 'country clubs', Rotary, British Legion, CIU (Working Men's Clubs), etc. They range between some which are clearly profit-making businesses (for example, Redwood Lodge Country Club near Bristol) to those which are non-profit-making (for example, the British Legion). They also range between those that are almost totally open in their membership (for example, most squash centres) to those which are quite restricted (for example, the CIU). Such private centres may run their own single-activity clubs or may act simply as a venue for outside groups.

Our second category comprises meeting rooms in pubs and other buildings. The Kingswood Military Modelling Association meets in premises owned by the furniture makers' trade union.

Churches form the third group and often provide space to a wide variety of groups, some church-related (for example, the Mothers' Union), others merely branches of major, national church-generated organizations such as the Methodist Association of Youth Clubs. Some groups may be linked through local members to that church while still others (for example, the Kingswood Photographic Society) are merely external renters of space.

The fourth category is firms' pitches and premises. On a statistical level they must be the second largest national provider of sports pitches and many firms still run extensive premises with pools, meeting rooms, bars, etc., at least as good as anything elsewhere. As with private clubs, many distinct teams operate within this framework, although by no means all the players are employees, ex-employees or have ever been employed by that firm. A worrying issue is the speed with which many firms are withdrawing from this type of support and often selling land and buildings.

Sponsorship

This issue – the direct or indirect provision of cash aid on a regular or *ad hoc* basis – is of increasing importance for groups throughout the leisure world, even though it originated from top-level professional activity in sport. National sponsorship is now well established – 'Benson and Hedges' in cricket, other major firms for concert series or art exhibitions. It now occurs regularly at regional level (the Sun Life Western Hockey League or the Bowdens Cricket League, for example) and is filtering down to local support (for example, the Bendix Band in Kingswood).

While John Player will support motor racing for reasons of direct advertisement, this rarely seems true for regional support. Here the sponsorship is more about a broad development of a company's image and reputation within a labour market (raising the question of whether companies are now shifting investment into sponsorship and away from direct provision via their own pitches and premises). Thus Sun Life Assurance consciously sought a vehicle for sponsorship after moving to Bristol a few years ago. In terms of what to sponsor, a company such as Sun Life has a clear strategy. There are 'taboos' – anything too closely associated with drinking, for example – and preferences – especially sports. They also prefer both to sponsor at a level synonymous with their employment market (that is, sub-regional) and to avoid sponsoring one group. Bendix, however, a firm with a small employment catchment area, chose to support a youth band in their immediate locality, almost regardless of standard.

The other aspect of sponsorship is its regularity. Much sponsorship for sports leagues is for three to five years, providing cash for a calendar of events, printed material, balls, stickers and so forth; all very carefully accounted. Other support can be *ad hoc*, for specific events such as exhibitions, shows and festivals and much of this can be very low key – typically paying for what is probably a useless advertisement in the programme.

The public sector

There are several quite different ways in which the practices of local authorities can impinge upon the groups in their areas, and by no means all of these occur through the more obvious departments (in Kingswood, for example, the grants to local groups are handled by the administration department). It is significant, however, to remember that the whole area of public leisure policy is in a considerable state of flux.

The first contribution made by the public sector is through the provision of pitches and premises. Although the pattern was less simple in Kingswood, the majority of groups in Kingswood and Leicester that we encountered used local authority pitches or premises, provided either by district or county councils. In Kingswood more groups were likely to own their pitches – perhaps reflecting the longer-established wealth of the area – or to gain access to them through the community associations, themselves often using some public support.

The degree of 'control' exerted by groups over pitches and premises can vary considerably. Some groups almost consider themselves to be the 'owners' and Bristol City Council, for example, has recently agreed that a football club can build its own premises on a council-owned pitch. Towards the middle of the spectrum are many groups who have 'always' used a pitch or a hall, yet in fact only book it yearly or quarterly with no real guarantee of continuity. Still other groups have a tenuous hold over pitch or space and must continuously reassert their rights.

A final issue is charges. The cost of pitches has risen dramatically in recent years' and yet, despite complaints from groups, the combined fees from what might be two winters and one summer user are probably still much less than the real cost to the authority. The assertive independence of groups may not always be as great as they imagine and many would find it difficult to keep going if it were not for the covert subsidy they receive when using local authority facilities. Other recent developments within the public sector also have a bearing on the autonomy of communal leisure groups. Only a few years ago the notion of recreation management was unknown; groups would always use the pitch they started with, park keepers would often be a law unto themselves and new groups would have to struggle to find a venue. Now, however, local authority managers in charge of swimming pools, sports centres, etc., are becoming more conscious of the many difficult choices to be made when allocating public sector resources.

Localism

Bristol City Council has a current policy to develop 'local' sports centres and yet has no local management policy. Thus most users of inner city centres are not in fact from those areas; a contrast with Newcastle where local centres are managed with firm discrimination in favour of local groups and individuals. We have given the example of the Matthews Morris group and their use of space perhaps needed by a new, local group, yet we have also argued that many groups cannot and should not be strictly local. The localist perspective does, however, appear to be on the increase and can militate against some groups.

Casual/regular users

It is almost certainly true that most centres could be filled at peak times entirely by formally constituted groups, leaving no space for casual users. This would give safe, regular, low-supervision uses but less income. We know of no centre run in this manner, which must reflect a view of the relative value of casual as compared to arranged activity.

Existing/latent groups

It seems possible that one factor inhibiting the emergence of new groups may well be the problems of finding space or a pitch. Equally it is difficult for a manager to argue preference for a new and potentially fragile group and to eject a well-established booking. On this issue we suspect that management decisions are sometimes influenced in favour of the 'easiest option', namely, existing provision.

Pricing

We have already suggested that casual users pay more than club members for use of the same local authority facilities, yet their demand is more erratic and they require more supervision. Given existing levels of subsidization, groups may over the coming years bear the greater brunt of increases in charges. Not surprisingly many groups are, at the moment, finding economic survival very difficult. The prognosis looks worrying.

Another way in which the public sector intervenes is through its staff, and not exclusively those in leisure and recreation departments. It can include personnel from education, social services, housing, youth service, parks, planning and various central departments. Naturally those from leisure and recreation work full-time on such issues, though we detect a general emphasis for such workers to focus on sport rather than crafts or hobbies. For most other people, the leisure link will be far more of a general community development role, although it should also be remembered that Leicester City Council calls its outposted recreation and arts workers 'Community Development Officers'.

The impact of such staff varies from very rare aid and advice to a major initiation role (as with Southfields Dynamos). Typical might be a worker for Kingswood District who advertised for people interested in forming a netball team, ran an open meeting, helped with pitches, equipment and organization and then left well alone. Achieving an impact on existing groups, with their often fierce sense of independence, seemed far more problematic.

A similar reaction from groups was obvious when we examined another means of intervention – grants. In our research we experienced examples of grants for buildings, equipment, publicity, events, trips away, or even to subsidize tickets in order to widen an 'audience'. The 'ground rules' for amounts, purposes, decided by whom, at what time of the year, with what regularity, with what strings attached, can vary considerably. As grants to voluntary bodies in Leicester have increased as part of the Urban Programme, so has the amount of bureaucracy necessary to take decisions and ensure public accountability for the direction, purpose and ultimate effectiveness of monies spent. In smaller districts such as Kingswood, however, it is likely that little money is available, limits may be as low as £200 and decisions are taken once a year by the local sports and arts councils.

The key difference, however, between Leicester and Kingswood was that the majority of grants in the former went to new groups while, in Kingswood, grants went to established, changing and new groups. This emphasizes the feelings of independence of groups and their sense that any pecuniary association with the local authority would mean some sort of loss of autonomy. The Oldville Players, for example, desperate for £200 to buy some new lights, were appalled at the idea of approaching 'the council', almost as if it were charity. The word 'interference' was used on occasion during interviews and there is in fact some anecdotal evidence that one form of such support – through the Manpower Service Commission – does indeed alter the character and nature of groups receiving that support.

The final contribution of the public sector is more properly thought of as intermediary between the authority and the local community. It is through local arts or sports councils. While not strictly a local authority function, many such councils are administered by that authority and use its premises for meetings. Membership is commonly local councillors, representatives of local groups or leagues and a servicing local government officer. We had little opportunity to examine such groups in detail and can only report *ad hoc* comments because these were invariably of a similar type. The impression given was that the councils are dominated by the more popular activities and the larger organizations, not allowing enough consideration of, for example, lapidarism or handball because no representative was on the council. It was felt that such councils are not wide enough in their representation, a further indicator of the sub-cultural independence of many groups.

Public sector involvement in leisure is currently undergoing some quite major changes. Recent years have seen the formation of the Institute of Leisure and Amenity Management as an amalgamation of four previously quite small and separate professional associations.* This amalgamation can probably be considered both a result of and a reason for the emergence of new, coherent, corporate departments within local government. The precise nature of these continues to vary between authorities, but might typically cover parks development and maintenance, indoor sports and leisure, arts development and premises management, allotments, open space,

---

* An interesting combination of the Institute of Park and Recreation Administration, the Association of Recreation Managers, the Institute of Municipal Entertainment and the Institute of Recreation Management.

even environmental improvement and (as in Leicester) aspects of community development. The ILAM is also attempting to consolidate its development as a new, single profession by establishing a primarily graduate intake using its own agreed courses and qualifications.

All of the above would seem, especially to the casual observer of previously very disparate local authority practices, to be a welcome shift. In many senses this is true, given the rise in status of 'leisure' generally and the consequent need for positive developmental work and the management of potentially overburdened facilities. In relation to our own subject matter, however, there are some areas of concern, to which we return in our final chapter.

The independent sector

This section may appear small in relation to those covering the commercial and public sectors, but it is nonetheless of considerable importance.

While not many areas would be able to offer as many independent establishments as Kingswood[6] (with its seven major community associations), this example merely serves to illustrate one end of the spectrum. At the opposite end one would find establishments – such as many community centres – which are funded and controlled primarily by the public sector. Naturally it is only at the former end of the spectrum that one can assert that the premises are provided independently (even if often grant-aided), but we consider that premise provision is only a secondary benefit for the groups.

The most significant contribution of the independent sector is, from our experience, to be found in the quality of support it offers to groups – and this can be equally true at either end of our spectrum. This support also does not have to be direct and practical to be of value. The key point is that any individual group should be able to see some form of organization or federation with which it can become involved, comprised primarily of groups like themselves – composed of enthusiasts rather than community professionals, public officers or councillors. This is almost certain to apply in centres such as those in Kingswood, but can also occur even within strongly public sector funded establishments. Naturally such committees or associations can and do provide practical help (as can a 'Leisure Services Officer') though we would repeat that their major value lies in a form of solidarity and mutuality, but on this occasion between groups rather than amongst individuals.

This completes the description of the many factors which impinge upon groups from outside and which can serve either to inhibit or encourage them. In order to provide more concrete examples of the issues discussed above, we will examine two examples of what we term 'intermediary' organizations – one a community association from Kingswood, the other a community college from Leicester. Each represents a different approach to intervention but the key issues of autonomy, independence, subsidy and support are illustrated in both.

Conwood Folk Centre

As you enter the Conwood Folk Centre, the immediate impression is of various activities taking place in a number of rooms, some of which are not easy to find. It is possible to find the main hall being used for a drama rehearsal, the bridge club in an upper room, a ladies' keep-fit class underway, snooker being played and at least one committee fighting its way through an agenda. The bar will probably not be very full yet; it fills up as some of the groups (they call them 'sections') finish their meetings. As a visitor or new arrival you would have to ask your way, but a 'regular' may well ask if you need help. That 'regular' may be a section member, the secretary or even the warden, who is a full-time employee stationed at the centre by the county council.

This is one of the seven very different Kingswood Community Associations. What are its roots? How and why does it function? Is it one association or a 'federation' of groups? In our studies we gleaned a fairly good if somewhat partial view of this organism and its current concerns.

The centre was started after the Second World War by a group of people who 'wanted to do something for the district'. The association was formed and, quite quickly, bought some land in Conwood for £3,500 – a considerable sum then. The constitution was established at that time and survives today with no major changes. After using ex-army huts for some years, they received a grant from Gloucestershire County Council and built a hall, a lounge and a snooker room. The impression given by these older members is of a much smaller organization operating within a much more tightly knit community than today: 'it was very much a village community, quite distinct from Kingswood'. There were clearly a few key families at the time, but many people became involved in a variety of activities in order to sustain the overall identity of the centre. Most original members became involved in the management of their 'sections' and then, very quickly, with the centre management as a whole.

Today there are over 900 members, all of whom have to join first a 'section' and then the association – although there are perhaps fifty purely 'social' members who use the bar regularly. Not all groups using the buildings however are sections, some (for instance, the Conwood Naturalists) are merely outside lettings. At the time of the research there were twenty-seven sections covering a variety of activities.

The hockey, cricket and tennis clubs mainly use the sports ground a couple of miles down the road, with its own changing rooms and bar, but often have their committee meetings at the main building. The local technical college also uses the centre on occasions for evening classes. As well as regular meetings of each section, each holds some management meetings there as well as occasional events such as exhibitions (for example, photography or dance). There is also an annual fair and some Christmas events and dances, etc.

Although the activities appear fairly wide-ranging, there is nothing for youth groups, nothing specifically for retired men, for the unemployed or for younger people generally. Nevertheless there is, as we have suggested, a good buzz of activity on most days of the year.

How, then, is this organization managed? A warden is appointed by the county council (the Community Services section of the Education Department) to the centre on a full-time basis, but in a role that includes outreach to the surrounding community as well as working directly on behalf of the centre. This appointment is not, however, imposed upon the centre. All the Kingswood District centres have a choice of whether or not to accept a warden. Apart from a caretaker paid by the association, the warden is the only true and non-voting place on the management committee. The latter is just one of four committees which run the centre: sports ground committee (responsible for the pitches, tennis courts and pavilion); social committee (responsible primarily for the bar but also general social activities); management committee (policy-making and widely representative); and executive committee (the final action-taking body).

Although the social committee plays a major role through bar profits, the example of another centre a few miles away is often quoted to show the dangers of creating a primarily social club – what is termed a mere drinking club. At this other centre the bar is the focus, activities are very exclusive, and moves towards a wider community role are resisted, to the extent that the offer from the county of a full-time warden was refused. By contrast, in Conwood there is a strong feeling that the community side should take precedence over the social side. This is partly achieved by emphasizing the sections at the expense of the overall centre.

The management committee comprises about twenty-five to thirty people who effectively decide the policy for the centre. They include the officers, trustees (some of whom are no longer active section members), general members elected at the AGM and representatives from parish and district councils. The general members are not on the committee as representatives of their section and this point was made several times. A representative system is deliberately avoided because 'the management committee is there to make sure the Folk Centre is run along the right lines', as the chairman put it. It is argued that representatives would do no more than press the views of each section. In reality most sections appear to be represented although there has generally been a majority from one or other section. At the moment it is moving from a preponderance of drama members to one of cricket club members. The management committee meets monthly but generally only with around fifteen people present.

The need for balance between the sections and the overall association is considered vital by most committee members. On the one hand, they have to draw the sections into the overall running of the community association. As one trustee argued, 'There isn't a wonderful set of people called "they" who run the centre; it's "you" not "they".' On the other hand, they have to keep a check on 'sectionalism'. As another committee member put it, 'A simple form of representation could lead to them becoming just a letting agency. More and more you've got to be looking at it all as a unit, a leisure unit rather than as separate things.'

The executive committee comprises all the officers, the community worker (warden), trustees and a minutes secretary. Their role is to implement the decisions of the management committee, but they quite evidently also take their own decisions. Here again the tense relationship between the centre and its sections emerges. While the management committee, by virtue of its wide representation, can have some influence over sections, the executive feel constantly unsure about directing sections to do anything, preferring to 'suggest' things to them.

The first of the three current issues which serve to raise questions about the relative value of 'parts' and 'whole' is very practical and concerns all those many jobs which have to be undertaken to make a complex building work successfully. As any member of a club probably realizes, a key but routine task is staffing the bar and canteen. While this issue was widely recognized it clearly raised deeper concerns, as the following two comments made by executive committee members illustrate: 'The way the community looks at the Folk Centre is changing. Whereas it used to be a community thing, it has now got so big that it really is becoming more of a leisure centre where you go and do your own thing. It is only the older people who are more community-oriented who join the management committee.

We are on our knees trying to get volunteers in the canteen and particularly behind the bar.' 'I think you've got a small nucleus of people who are prepared to run community centres, clubs, whatever, and work for them. You've got a lot of people who will use them if it suits their purposes. It's a pity there aren't more willing to help. Now we're almost looking to the local authority to do everything.'

One concomitant of creating a centre which is merely an assembly of independent parts is that tasks such as staffing the bar begin to take on the character we described earlier as that of traditional voluntary work, that is, no longer working for yourself or your group but for 'them'. As the warden pointed out, members were still happy to do this for those defined as in 'need' (old people, the disabled, etc.) but not for a general body of members.

The second element contributing to change was the new extension. Space had become very limited and a decision had been taken to add a new small hall, expand the bar, improve the canteen and add another meeting room. The actual planning of the extension was fairly easy. The design was done by the architect husband of a member. Gaining grants proved more problematic. The centre had over £35,000 in reserve for the task and asked Kingswood District Council for another £25,000. They seemed well placed to get the grant, but the available money for one year went to another centre amidst rumours of 'shady' lobbying. Nevertheless they received the grant the following year and are now building.

At the moment, most groups at the centre are well established and have had access to their set time and venue for many years. With new spaces available, two difficult decisions lie ahead. First, do they choose to leave groups where they are currently or reallocate them to make better use of the space? Second, do they also (or alternatively) choose to bring in or promote entirely new activities which will extend the range of activities? They could, for example, choose only to expand existing groups and leave them all where they are. At another extreme, they could choose to bring in several new groups and move around several of the existing groups. Some of the new groups could be specifically for young people, as some committee members wish.

The drama group who currently meet every Friday in the large hall only take up part of the space, exemplifying the management problems. They need the large area for final rehearsals and performances but sometimes only five people attend on a Friday evening. They have also added many things to improve the stage, paid for by themselves but obviously of benefit to all. Should they be moved to another night (Friday being a prime time for activities) and/or to the new small hall? Will the management committee 'grasp this nettle'?

Due to policy changes within the county, the role of the warden has reverted far more strongly to that of a general community worker based at the centre but developing many more external links. She was especially concerned about the potentially very parochial and exclusive nature of many groups, but also suspected that the same applied to the centre as a whole in relation to the wider community: 'When I get out into the community I have the label of Conwood Folk Centre put around me and I am not seen as a community worker. I think that has worked perhaps against me. We are very aware that the name Folk Centre does promote an image of the older generation.' She was very unsure how the centre committees would react (especially given that they will lose some of her time) if she were to start up a club in a nearby church hall. She would, through such work, be giving more of her time to seeking out 'latent' demand or even 'need' within the community – some elements of which may be very antagonistic to the centre – rather than helping, supporting and developing existing groups. There is thus a tension between a wide community development role, the needs of an intermediary organization such as the community association and the needs of individual groups – a tension not easily resolved.

Thurnley Community College

Leicestershire's network of community colleges is undoubtedly the closest equivalent in that area to the community associations of Kingswood. We were fortunate in that one of the county's community colleges, Thurnley, operated within our study area in north-east Leicester.

The essential difference between Kingswood's community associations and Leicestershire's community colleges is that whereas the former arose as independent initiatives of local people which, as they have grown, have to some extent become enmeshed within local authority policy and practice, the community colleges were from the outset a public sector initiative which has developed in a progressively decentralized manner. Not surprisingly, therefore, the key issues facing local authority personnel operating out of Conwood and Thurnley are quite different, indeed almost contrary. Whereas at Conwood the community worker is faced with the difficulty of overcoming a parochialism which might militate against the Folk Centre ever becoming more than simply a sum of its parts, at Thurnley the community education officers are faced with the opposite difficulty, how to transfer power from the professional, public sector officers to local groups so that the process of decentralization can take real shape and form.

The Thurnley Community College is very much an example of 'dual use' policies in action. During the daytime the community college is in fact a comprehensive secondary school. During the evening and at weekends all of its facilities – halls, workshops, gym, playing fields, etc. – are available for use by adult education classes or local groups.

Whilst the community college initially took on the character of a centre for adult education, over the last five years in particular it has shifted away from a focus upon conventional forms of adult education towards self-managed forms of community education. This shift in focus has occurred partly by design and partly by accident.

On the 'design' side there can be little doubt that a core group of staff and governors share a common vision in which the college is seen as the vehicle through which the boundaries between child and adult education, and between the college and the community, will eventually be broken down. This strategy has, however, also been assisted by 'accident' – notably the unforeseen cutbacks in educational expenditure which were particularly severe in the late 1970s and early 1980s. The 1980 cutbacks seemed likely to undermine severely the programme of evening classes that the college provided at that time. A well-supported meeting was held for all those attending evening classes at the college to discuss the cuts and from the floor an innovative tactic began to emerge to mitigate the impact of cuts. It was suggested that many of the more established classes could become affiliated clubs, taking on responsibility for their own training and development or, where appropriate, paying former 'tutors' on an honorarium basis. As a result, many former classes became clubs or societies. Since then many new groups have been formed as people began to prefer the format of the club to that of the class. A reduced programme of evening classes still exists (many activities such as typing/shorthand are not amenable to the 'club' format) and other activities (for instance, yoga) continue some years as formal classes and other years as informal clubs, depending upon how many people enroll. Of one thing there can be no doubt, however; over the last five or six years the gross amount of evening and weekend activities has grown considerably.

As a result of this development, the management committee of the community college is now dominated numerically by representatives from the affiliated groups. In addition the management committee includes representatives from the evening classes, the chairperson of the Board of Governors, the principal of the college, the two community education officers, representatives of the college's 'outstations' (that is, local primary schools within this community education area) and other relevant professional officers (for example, local youth workers). There are no separate sub-committees. Club use of playing field and gym facilities long pre-dates 1980 and any problems regarding bookings, etc., are sorted out directly by the community education officers.

The management committee has its own devolved budget. Income from letting of facilities now exceeds £25,000 per annum, of which 20 per cent is clawed back by the County Education Department, the remainder going directly into the management committee budget. Using this income, the management committee subsidizes affiliated groups by helping them with the purchase of equipment and has put finance into major projects such as a college minibus and a bar. The acquisition of a bar has been a key event in the history of most of the community associations in Kingswood. The possibilities of generating income through bar profits are substantial and there can be little doubt that the bar and its associated social facilities has proved central to the rapid development of many of Kingswood's community associations. On the other hand a successfully run bar inevitably poses certain problems, not the least of which is the legal requirement to establish a bar or social committee which, once formed, often aspires to demand some say over how bar profits are used. In the case of Thurnley this kind of problem is unlikely to arise for some time – the bar has been open for eight months now but usage is still comparatively slight. Perhaps there are real limits to 'dual use' strategies – a building which has been designed primarily for education rather than leisure offers a rather bleak prospect for potential social drinkers.

As with the Conwood Folk Centre the key issues regarding the operation of the Thurnley Community College and its management committee relate to the question of power and control. Unlike Conwood, there can be no doubt that the community groups, despite their numerical superiority, are a relatively powerless element of the Thurnley management committee. We were able to attend the 1984 AGM of the management committee and, though well attended by group representatives, it was nevertheless dominated by a small number of education department officers – the community education officers, detached youth worker and so forth. The chairperson of the management committee (a member of the Thurnley Community Orchestra), was re-elected unopposed even though he admitted, when interviewed afterwards, that he felt very uncomfortable in the post. In his own words he had previously protested to one of the community education officers that there were other professionals 'who I'm sure, would make a better job of it than me'. Nevertheless this officer 'insisted it should be a layman.' Whilst it is difficult to know how representative the AGM was of other management committee meetings, the way in which the chairman's role was performed at this meeting left much to be desired. The two community education officers sat on either side of the chairman and, throughout the length of the meeting, passed him messages, whispered instructions to him and, on several occasions, openly interrupted and more or less took over the chairmanship from him. Clearly their intention was to be supportive, but the effect was a bizarre display in which the actual chairman was made to appear a puppet.

The chairman is a self-employed engineer, a quiet and rather humble, middle-aged man who appears fairly unsuited to the task with which he has found himself confronted. The previous chairman was a retired industrial consultant and member of the National Executive of the British Association of Beekeepers. He became involved with the college through his wife who was in the Art Club. It seemed that he quickly became involved on the management side of things, even though he was not himself a member of any constituent group within the college. Obviously a man familiar with the conduct of meetings, he soon became chairperson of the management committee, resigning his post two years ago when appointed chairperson of the college Board of Governors. He still attends management committee meetings, but in his new role; indeed, he was one of the few who did dominate proceedings at the AGM.

The fact that he (the previous chairman) has not himself been involved with any of the groups that use Thurnley is betrayed by a number of opinions à-regarding the role of the groups *vis-à-vis* the college. Whilst he shared the vision of overcoming the boundary between child and adult education, he seemed less enthusiastic than the community education officers about breaking down the barrier between the college and the community. He criticized the groups for failing to participate in his own broad vision; their main role (from his point of view) being to make demands. He did not feel that it is the role of the management committee to hand out money to groups.

The contrast with Conwood Folk Centre could not be greater. There the community groups were everything, and the concept of the Folk Centre as a corporate unit playing a co-ordinated role in the development of the community was little more than a hope for a few relatively powerless individuals no longer closely tied to 'sections'. At Thurnley the groups are not without influence but power is enjoyed primarily by a small group of professional officers and a group of what might be termed the 'professional laity'. We use this phrase to describe what tends to happen to local activists who become incorporated into the management and operation of decentralized aspects of the local authority and who, in the process, adopt the perspective of the professionalized public sector rather than that of the community and its organizations (from whence they come). Besides the former chairman we might mention the woman who runs the bar in this category. She has been active in the Rushey Fields area ever since the new estate was built there (over six years ago). Until the most recent AGM she was secretary of the management committee but has now become so heavily involved in establishing the bar at the community college that one of the community education officers announced her resignation (apparently without consulting her) as he felt the two tasks were too much for her to undertake!

Prompted strongly by its ex-chairman and some of the education officers, the management committee is now focusing most of its resources on the creation of a 'youth wing' at the college. The project will cost the management committee upwards of £20,000, assuming an equivalent contribution from the county education authority. Interestingly enough, requests from groups for financial assistance hardly obtained any consideration at the AGM nor, apparently, were they considered at the previous meeting of the management committee. It was this absence which prompted the present chair of the management committee, in a rare display of autonomy, to remind those present that the affiliated groups are the meat and body of the thing... support to the groups needs to be there'.

The committee has, in the past, used its financial resources to buy a large number of micro-computers and electric typewriters primarily for the school's use. The minibus is also heavily used by the school, though the bar, for obvious reasons, is not. Thus one forms the impression of a community college having gained for itself considerable devolved budgetary powers (powers that the county education authority are now trying to undermine in a variety of minor ways), but which nevertheless exercises these powers in such a way that the constituent groups tend to gather the leftovers rather than the lion's share of the resources. A dialogue of sorts exists between the professionals and the laity, though undoubtedly a great deal of this dialogue takes place indirectly through the small group of 'professionalized laity' that we identified earlier. Many affiliated clubs, particularly users of the gym and playing fields, have little or no contact with the management committee, even though as affiliated clubs they are entitled to send a representative. The management committee meets irregularly (its AGM was in January 1984, the two previous management committee meetings had occurred in September and June in 1983) and though well attended by group representatives we were left with the strong impression that such representatives participated in – without determining – the frame-work within which business was conducted. As one community education officer suggested, the 'management committee is a very good sounding board'. In other words, despite its title, it is still essentially a consultative committee. At the same time, there can be no doubting the sincerity of the two community education officers in seeking to proceed further down the path towards real community involvement and control.

In retrospect, therefore, a superficial organizational description of Conwood Folk Centre and Thurnley Community College could convey the impression of two very similar bodies. We have shown, however, that the directions from which each has come, the future routes they might follow and the general 'feel' of each is in fact very different. The crucial dimensions are, however, clear and common – the balance between the 'parts' and the 'whole', 'stability' versus 'community development' and the role of central 'organizers' – be they professional or 'incorporated laity'.

Chapter 7

The structure and dynamic of communal leisure organizations

In this chapter we wish to examine the underlying structure of communal leisure organizations, in order to gain a more profound understanding of their dynamics. The cameos of Chapter 2 have provided a fairly detailed description of a few of these groups, but will not have revealed whether there are any common patterns or dynamics observable across all such groups. How democratic are such groups in general? Do they tend towards being cliquish? Are they dogged by conflicts, bickering and rivalries? As we shall see, the answers are rarely simple.

Despite the impact of sub-cultural influences, the varying interests and values that members bring, the impingements of local authority leisure officers and community workers, the difficulties in obtaining access to desired facilities and so forth, what impressed us was the ability of groups to retain a very clear and distinctive identity, one which was clearly more than the sum of the contributions of specific members at a specific time. The majority of groups were able to offer sharp 'thumbnail' sketches both of themselves and others with whom they come into contact, distinguishing each quite clearly.

How is this sense of identity achieved? To begin our investigation we must return to Chapter 3. One cannot begin to understand the nature of communal leisure organizations without first acknowledging their distinctive character as forms of mutual aid. The purpose of the Charnwood Aquarists, the Monktonians, etc., is not to serve others, but to serve themselves. If in the course of doing this they give others pleasure, this is a fortunate by-product. They are groupings of enthusiasts whose primary purpose, dread the thought, is to enjoy themselves. Of course within a particular club participants will obtain their pleasure in different ways. Within Conwood Hockey Club some gained most pleasure through winning, some through busying themselves with the organization of the club, some simply from the opportunity to play. Others undoubtedly got most out of the social side of the club's activities while a few, apparently, were motivated by the more amorous possibilities inherent in playing mixed hockey. Self-organized communal leisure provides people with many different forms of enjoyment, together with the opportunity to consume what they themselves have created. It is this that undoubtedly provides the key to the strong sense of identity within groups.

It would be mistaken to conclude that, because such organizations are formed by people freely associating to enhance each others' pleasure, they resemble participatory collectives. In most of the clubs we looked at, the organization of the group was undertaken by a small minority of the members. Indeed, the vast majority of members would not even turn up to the club's AGM if they could possibly avoid it. Yet, surprisingly, this sharp division of labour was very often the actual basis for a sense of collective solidarity, of a shared identity. How are we to make sense of this?

After a while we began to realize that what separates a mutual aid organization from other kinds of organization is the perception by members that even where the club's organization lies in the hands of 'the same old few, year after year', they are perceived as being a part of 'us'. Thus, subjectively speaking, within mutual aid the organization of the group is nearly always performed 'by some of us, for all of us' and not 'by them, for us'. Here it is useful to think in terms of a continuum, rather than discrete categories.

At one end of the continuum the task of organization is an integral part of the enthusiasm itself. Everyone in the club helps out with its organization, as was more or less the case with the Matthews Morris Men. There may well be discrete organizational roles – bagman, squire – but there is no obvious group of participants who are not also organizers. A little further along this continuum one can find groups, which are perhaps slightly larger, in which the majority of participants contribute to the organization. Thus Redland Ladies' Hockey Club, which ran just two teams, was organized by a committee of sixteen. As the secretary disarmingly noted, 'We've got over half the club down there. We don't really make any great decisions at a meeting. I suppose people like to get together for a chat.' Yet further along one encounters clubs such as the Charnwood Aquarists where the organization is run by a (largish) minority of members with regular changes of personnel; and further still one sees Conwood Hockey Club where the distance between the committee and the majority of members is wider. In the case of Conwood, what would happen if the oldest members stopped playing but continued to work on the committee? This is what happens in most local football clubs and many cricket clubs. In soccer the vast majority of chairmen, secretaries, treasurers, etc., are players who have 'hung up their boots' but who retain a strong involvement with their club. Here the division of labour within the group has proceeded one step further – most organizers are not players and most players are not organizers, yet the players continue to perceive that the organization is undertaken 'by some of us, for all of us'.

Imagine what would happen if local community workers tried to rescue a club in crisis by taking over these organizational roles. Almost certainly the nature of the club would change as players would perceive that the club was now being run 'by them, for us'. We are almost at the end of our continuum: those groups in which the distinction between organizer and participant is so considerable that we feel it may be legitimate to speak of the 'voluntary work' of the organizers who do things 'for others'. Such a situation often occurs when a mutual aid organization is on the point of collapse. As the secretary of a football club in Leicester said to us, 'I've had enough now, especially when you don't get help from other people. There's only one person on this committee I can guarantee will help me. The others don't want to be dedicated.' This final point on our continuum also corresponds to the normal pattern of organization in children's leisure – virtually all amateur swimming clubs, youth football clubs, etc., are organized by adults on behalf of children.

The football secretary's complaint reveals the nature of the tie which binds members of mutual aid groups together, despite the often considerable division of labour within them. The tie is based upon the principle of reciprocity – a key element in what is sometimes called 'the gift relationship', a form of relationship which is direct and unmediated by calculation. Take a typical cricket club like the Downend Club. Their Second Team will be watched by a handful of spectators who will probably consist of a couple of committee members, a few co-players and the odd relative. The club itself is, by and large, the product of these people and a few other organizers. The performance of the team on the pitch is the product of the collective labour of the eleven cricketers. Just as the players appreciate the work of the organizers in giving them a club to play for, so the organizers appreciate the work of the players in giving their best on the pitch. And at the end of the match players and supporters of the opposing teams will thank each other (usually by a ritual handshake) for their respective contributions to the match. Social relationships between organizers and players, players and spectators, players and players are therefore not mediated by any market expectations.

Of course reciprocity has its darker side as well. The gift may be a 'poisoned gift';[1] for instance, the organizers may only give on condition of receipt and the players may be made to feel permanently indebted to those who have 'made the club possible'. But even in cases such as these, social relationships still assume the form of 'gift relationship' rather than 'commercial relationship'. As Gershuny notes when speaking of the informal economy:

What distinguishes this category of production is that real money is not used as an indicator of exchange of value for value. Where money is paid it is explicitly not in exchange for value received – so officers of communal organisations are paid *honoraria, in recognition not exchange for services,* and expenses, although they may be fiddled, are rarely used as complete compensation.[2] [Our emphasis.]

We have tried to convey a picture of some of the defining characteristics of communal leisure organizations – their strong sense of identity, of 'us-ness', the role of reciprocity as a way of binding individuals to the group despite their different contributions. Let us explore further.

We would suggest that there can be two levels of analysis of any communal leisure group. First, there are some *surface characteristics* such as membership, finance, constitution, formal committee structure and so forth. However, it should be clear to anyone with even the most brief experience of a hockey club or dance group, for example, that such simple facts and figures hide much of the reality of how groups operate. Behind a statement by the secretary of a badminton club that the club takes 'any new member regardless of ability' are a series of unwritten rules and procedures which ensure that 'inappropriate' applicants go elsewhere or that they are suitably vetted on their arrival. Almost without exception, the simple, black and white rules revealed in response to our questionnaire became complex and also far richer the moment we started discussing them with somebody in a particular group. It is this *deeper structure* of the organization which offers the best guide to the true nature and identity of any group. Here we can observe the methods by which groups handle the many conflicting inputs we have described earlier while still operating at a level of formal consistency (typically a constitution) which enables them to participate in their chosen activity with others. It is the level at which the formal rules (or assumed social conventions) are 'humanized' to relate to individual needs.

The distinction between surface characteristics and the hidden structure and culture of a group is of the utmost importance. We hardly encountered one organization where the formal constitution and/or committee structure was not perfectly democratic, yet if one went beyond the surface one discovered enormous variations – from the Conwood Hockey Club where the president and chairman constituted an awe-inspiring partnership, to an organization such as the Warmley Golden Hours (a self-organized group for pensioners) where the organizers appeared to be held in the powerful grip of a passive membership. The official organizational structure tells you very little about the actual distribution of power. To locate a group's difficulties in its formal structure is, very often, to make the most profound mistake. We will return to this later on, but now we will look at some of the surface characteristics of communal leisure groups.

Surface characteristics

The data that we offer here refers to characteristics such as the size, type, age, etc., of a sample of seventy-one organizations in Kingswood and sixty-three in north-east Leicester. The information was gleaned primarily through a questionnaire, occasionally elaborated following personal contact.

Table 1 represents the explicit purpose of the groups.

Table 1

Area of interest	Kingswood		N E Leicester	
	No.	%	No.	%
Multi-function*	20	28	21	33
Sports	26	37	22	35
Arts	9	13	11	17
Crafts/hobbies	16	23	8	13
Miscellaneous	2	3	1	2

Note: * Multi-function refers to youth groups, Women's Institutes, OAP clubs, etc. We found that our figures appear to be surprisingly representative of the range of different forms of leisure activity which we obtained from our original trawl of nearly 300 groups in Kingswood and 230 in Leicester. The first thing to note is that sports constitute no more than a third of all leisure groups.

Table 2

Date	Kingswood	N E Leicester
Pre-1939	8	2
1939–70	28	15
1971–76	23	10
1977–82	10	35
No response	2	1

Regarding the date of formation of the groups, see Table 2. The most remarkable feature of Table 2 is the large number of fairly recently formed groups in Leicester, no doubt as a direct result of development work undertaken by the city's Recreation and Arts Department, together with the effect of the Urban Programme. Seventeen were formed in 1981 alone and this contrasts with the well-established pattern in Kingswood. It is possible that the 'youth' of groups in Leicester is some explanation of the variations in average membership between the two study areas as shown in Table 3.

Table 3

No.	Kingswood	N E Leicester
Maximum	855	475
Minimum	5	4
Average	90	54
Total	6,031	2,903
(Sample)	(67)	(54)

Table 3 shows Kingswood groups to be at least 50 per cent larger than those in Leicester and this divergence continues even when one removes the distorting effect of the few very large groups in each area (typically swimming clubs with 500–600 members). After removing these, the averages are fifty-three for Kingswood and thirty-six for Leicester.

On the subject of premises, we have mentioned the major contribution which is often made by local authorities either directly or indirectly to the provision of premises. In this respect our two study areas were very different in that Leicester's thrust came through local authority centres and community schools, while Kingswood's came through indirect support from largely independent community associations. Thus, in Table 4, the term 'passive schools' refers to situations where the schools merely let space, while 'active schools' denotes schools with a conscious community development role. 'Other institution' covers the many different forms of community association or semi-private establishments.

Table 4

Premises	Kingswood	N E Leicester
Local authority centres	16	30
Passive schools	4	6
Active schools	0	18

Church (and church use)	9	6
Church (non-church use)	6	3
Private	18	9
Other institution	31	2
Own premises	4	1
None	2	0
Other	0	2

The heavy reliance on district and county council intervention in Leicester is very obvious, as is the reliance on community associations in Kingswood. Our sampling was perhaps at its weakest with the small, semi-formal clubs such as dominoes, cribbage and darts, most of which would be expected to use private accommodation and hence alter these figures in both study areas.

On sources of finance our questionnaire offered a few specific choices and space for other suggestions. Table 5 reflects the fact that many groups use more than one method to attract funds. Subscription is clearly the most popular form of financing activity, although many groups undertake fund-raising events, often as much social as financial. The most popular format for subscriptions was a combination of an annual sum with some payment per meeting or match, thus ensuring support without too large a burden at any one point in the year.

Table 5

	Kingswood	N E Leicester
Subscriptions	64	51
Fund-raising	47	32
Grant	10	16
Grant only	1	2
Fund-raising only	1	1
No response	60	59

In terms of constitution, forty-five groups in Kingswood and thirty-two in Leicester had one, as opposed to twenty-two and twenty-nine without, usually the latter being the smaller and newer groups. From contact with the groups themselves we found great variations in practice for committees, membership, length of service, officers and so forth, although all within traditional democratic models. Perhaps the overwhelming response was from those in the onerous roles such as secretary or treasurer who had often occupied that role for some years. Their continued occupation of the role seemed more related to a lack of other possible candidates than to a desire to hold on to power.

Digging deeper

The mutual aid character of leisure groups finds direct expression in the structure and culture of these small organizations. As we have already indicated, we were particularly struck by the remarkably strong sense of identity that most of these leisure groups display, despite the diversity of interest and orientations their members bring. Such differences encourage the development of what could be seen as horizontal and vertical boundaries within the organization. The Charnwood Aquarists' Society, for example, is structured vertically according to whether members are 'cold water' or 'warm water' fish enthusiasts, competitive or non-competitive aquarists, 'live-bearing' fish breeders or 'egg-bearing' fish breeders, and so on. In addition, the organization will be structured horizontally according to whether one is part of the active group of organizers of the society or one of the ordinary members. In our experience leisure groups vary considerably in terms of involvement of members in the group's organization. We have already mentioned the drama society in which virtually all of its members appeared to be involved in its organization, and also the Ladies' Hockey Club with a committee the size of one and a half teams. At the opposite extreme, in many multi-function groups only a small minority are involved with organization.

Such examples suggest that, despite formal democratic structures, the character of a group is defined most powerfully by its culture – in this case whether the culture is participatory or non-participatory and dependent. Many organizations, like the Golden Hours Club, develop conscious strategies to compensate for their culture. For example, our cameo of the Monktonians described the way in which they held their AGM after a training session (which players would be expected to attend) in order to guarantee maximum involvement. However, many decisions and changes are achieved by default or unconsciously. Few groups 'choose' a particular balance between a professional approach to the activity or fun and enjoyment, or between participation and dependency. The majority of such processes are handled at an 'assumptive' or 'mundane'[3] world level which inevitably means that conflict and contradiction can stay hidden and potential is lost. While there are many very good reasons why no group should ever seriously consider opening each member's personal needs and motivations to group discussion, a lack of recognition of the interplay of such issues can lead to problems, perhaps to a member leaving unnecessarily. Such a lack of awareness can also lay a group open to deliberate manipulation by those few who are more aware of the forces at play, although, as we will demonstrate, most groups have 'fail-safe' mechanisms to defuse such manipulation.

The almost unconscious way in which many decisions are made in such communal leisure organizations is illustrated in the following account of the early life of the Southfields Dynamos in Leicester.

A number of youths, aged sixteen to twenty-two, got into the habit of having a 'kick-about' on a Saturday afternoon on some playing fields near the estate where they all lived. The estate, though fairly small, was the worst by far to be found in this Midlands city. At this stage the group was fairly open; anyone who knew an existing participant could come along. The most consistent attenders decided to constitute themselves as a club to enter a team for the city's Sunday League. They were surprised at the obligations involved in entering a league. The league insisted that they have two complete sets of kit, a formally constituted committee and a bank account. Through fund-raising activities, they met the league's requirements and after a formal interview they were allowed to enter the fourth division of the Sunday League the following September.

During the summer preceding their first season, they started regular training sessions. Training is encouraged but is not obligatory. Before the season had started, one team member announced that he had a cousin who lived some way away who was an excellent player and who was looking for a club to play for. Even though this player could not make training, he was given a regular place in the team because he was so good.

As the season progressed, the team found itself pushing for promotion. There were certain obvious weaknesses within the side, however. These were compensated for when an excellent goalkeeper (in his mid-thirties, but an ex-semi-professional) and two midfield players (one a relative and one a friend of an existing player) were obtained. None of the new players lived in the area. An older man from a local pub became the team manager.

By the end of the season, the team had finished third in the division (only the first two are promoted). There is a pool of sixteen players, including ten of the originals. However, only six of the originals consistently hold a place in the team. The Saturday afternoon 'kick-about' received lower and lower attendances, until by the end of the season it had been discontinued.

The key issue here concerns the way in which the club made a number of key choices, each choice leading the group in a slightly new direction. The problem is that more often than not these choices were made without full consideration of their possible consequences. The first and most obvious change to occur was the collective's objective which moved from being a non-competitive to a competitive one. The change in objective meant that the pattern of demands changed, essentially from a situation in which one made demands upon oneself to one in which the 'club' made increasing demands upon its 'members'. As the club began to import more and more 'outsiders', so it displaced more and more 'insiders'. This was acceptable while the kick-about sessions lasted, but when they declined a large number of the original collective were either not having their needs met at all or were only having them met in a restricting way – they had to accept formalized training, no sex on Saturday nights, a restriction on alcohol, for example.

There had obviously been a shift towards a more intensive form of need satisfaction. But was 'excellence' being pursued to the detriment of 'sport for all'?

Each choice, which marked a turning point in the history of the group, was made from a number of alternatives. The group could have decided not to become competitive. Having 'gone competitive' it could nevertheless have refused to invite players from outside. As organizations develop, they constantly encounter 'turning points' which crucially determine the future direction the group will take. The tragedy is that these turning points are often encountered (and passed) by an organization without it even having seen an alternative.

This example illuminates a central concern of some strands within modern organizational theory – namely, the 'mundane world' of the group or organization. Central to this notion is the idea that people in organizations quickly become embedded in a matrix of implicit and untested assumptions, hidden rules, rituals and myths, deep-structural rhythms, languages and orientations which carry them along as if they were the passive object of organizational process rather than its creative subject.

We suggest that there are several distinctive processes which groups use (perhaps unconsciously or by default) to cope with the diversity of their world. Some of these are concerned with the internal organization of any group: they learn how to cope with differences, they learn how to handle power and how best to utilize their human resources. Some of these processes are related to the negotiation of the group's boundary with its environment, to external pressures, including recruitment and induction. Moreover, because the internal world (rules, fees, etc.) does not remain the same for very long, groups have to find ways of coping with change.

Before moving on to examine the ways in which groups handle these issues, it would be useful to recap briefly on the essential elements of the deeper structure of such organizations. Within any communal leisure group boundaries will exist which are potential points of cleavage and conflict. Horizontal boundaries refer to the divide between organizers and organized, vertical boundaries refer to differences of interest and values between participants. If a group learns to negotiate these boundaries successfully, such differences will prove a source of enrichment; if it fails to handle them, then the divisions will harden and lead to the formation of cliques.

The two kinds of boundary often interact in a complex fashion. In an aquarists' society one is quite likely to find some members who prefer to specialize in 'live-bearer' fish and others who favour 'egg-bearers'. At another level, there will be some in the group who actively seek out some organizing role in whatever group they join or who are fairly easily persuaded, and others who would never seek to accept any role on a committee or even as an occasional organizer. It is not difficult to imagine the possible problems for the aquarists' society if only egg-bearer enthusiasts were willing to be on the committee (or deliberately packed it with representatives), or if national organizations decided to split dramatically and formed pressure groups to favour one type of fish or another. The way in which a group handles the differences in the interests and values of its membership is therefore crucial.

Handling differences

The Kingswood Military Modelling Society formed as a breakaway from the Bristol branch of the British Model Soldiers' Society. Here is an extract from an interview with their secretary:

> The breakaway group were originally figure men. By that I mean they paint people, although some do vehicle modelling. The average guy must go for Napoleonics – it's very colourful. One chap in our club does the Dark Ages, he knows a great deal about the Dark Ages, give him his due, he will argue with you on it for hours. Most members specialize. Our chairman doesn't. He does anything. It's incredible.

This extract not only gives an illustration of the diversity of interests within such a club (other specialists in the club concentrated on the Charge of the Light Brigade, scenic diorama work, wargaming, etc.), but something of its character: a kind of tolerant 'it takes all sorts' attitude. This is really what we mean by the culture of a group. Our respondent captured this particularly when referring to the club they broke away from.

> They are a bit regimented. Their meetings were a bit strict. You tended to get talked down to. Atmosphere is a funny thing to explain. Our meetings are a bit friendly; you get the impression there that the committee run everything. There's an ex-army officer down there. You get 'Hello, old boy!' and all that sort of gear.

The culture of a group therefore tends to express the collective values of its participants. The culture may be regimented, participative, competitive, sociable and so on. Very often such sets of values are non-exclusive; many highly professional and competitive clubs (like the Monktonians) will also be very sociable. Communal leisure groups therefore have to find ways of managing two different forms of diversity – in members' interests and in members' values. How do they achieve this? Our impression is that three approaches are available. First of all, care is taken to give formal representation to such differences on the club's committee. Secondly, great efforts are made to ensure that club activities reflect the balance of different interests. Thirdly, the recruitment and induction process is used as a way of controlling the diversity of group membership.

With regard to the formal representation of differences, one of the most common illustrations of this comes from amateur sport. Most sports clubs run several teams. In the case of the Conwood Hockey Club, for example, there were four teams, the captain of each being represented on the committee. In some instances (for example, Redland Ladies' Hockey) each team also has its own secretary who is on the main club committee. Lack of representation will often lead to tensions. The East Bristol Rifle and Pistol Club, for example, contained three main subsections – rifle, pistol and air weapons. According to the secretary, the club 'tries to specialize in rifles but unfortunately a few want to shoot pistols. In other clubs, pistol has tended to take over.' Another rifle shooter added, 'Our only problem is pistol shooters. I just wish they'd do it when I'm not there. It's a lot safer with rifle than pistol.' Whilst rifle shooters did not perceive a divide within the club, the pistol shooters did. Both the pistol captain and the air weapons captain are represented on the club's committee. There is, however, no rifle captain, rather there is a club captain – a source of great irritation to pistol and air weapons enthusiasts as the title more or less presupposes that it will be filled by a rifle enthusiast. At the same time, the Rifle and Pistol Club also take great care to provide a balance of activity within the club so that it can appeal to enthusiasts of all persuasions. Air weapons enthusiasts have their own small range to shoot from, pistol enthusiasts are allocated Friday night as their night (on other nights they have to seek the permission of rifle shooters to use the range). Our cameo of the Charnwood Aquarists' Society shows the same effort to provide a balance of activities and we have found this approach repeated in naturalist societies (alternating meetings on flora and fauna), lapidary societies, and so on.

Whilst toleration of differences is to some extent bound up with values, it is clearly on occasions something which is imposed rather than chosen. Undoubtedly East Bristol's Pistol Shooters would join a local pistol club if there were one available but, as there is not, they have to make the best of it. Nevertheless, splits often do occur and they clearly correspond to situations where differences have become unmanageable. According to the secretary of one of the amateur football leagues in Leicester, the majority of new clubs which apply to join his league are actually formed by players or organizers splitting off from existing clubs. Within the sphere of hobbies such splits are also common and are often based – as in the case of the Kingswood Military Modelling Society – on differences in values as much as differences in interests. Thus it is possible to see how important the process of recruitment and induction is in preserving the identity of groups.

Recruitment and induction processes

There can be little doubt that one major way in which groups cope with differences is by ensuring as far as is possible that the range of people, styles, approaches and skills within their groups are limited to a degree appropriate to a general conception of the group's purpose. Different groups will have very different perceptions of the amount of diversity they can, or wish to, contain. Thus a very large hockey club might nevertheless impose quite vigorous skill and fitness criteria, while a small club may be totally open to anybody wishing to play. Not surprisingly, most sports operate a fairly obvious system because standards of skill and fitness are easy to evaluate. In art, craft or hobby groups, however, it is far less clear cut and they tend to have a more open approach to new members. It becomes more difficult to judge more elusive notions such as competitiveness or commitment to organizational work. Hence the use of what we describe as an 'induction' process, often taking many months, during which a more rounded picture of any individual can be formed and he or she can also have time to adjust to the group.

Regarding selectivity, our experience suggests that 'entry rules' are actually very open in all but the elite groups of any activity. Moreover, we ought to reconsider the traditionally negative connotations of the word. This process is as much about the sustenance of a particular group and its identity than about exclusion and avoidance.

One simple way in which the recruitment process helps to preserve a group's identity where access is less open is through the use of wider social networks. Our account of the Southfields Dynamos illustrated how many of the club's new members were friends or relatives of the original group. In Chapter 5, where we examined the contribution of the individual enthusiast to the group, we noted how people very often joined groups for reasons which apparently had little to do with interest in the activity of the group itself – perhaps because friends 'dragged' them along. The use of social networks reduces the risk that new members for one reason or another 'won't fit'.

Consider the example of a rifle and pistol club. The club does not advertise for members, hence stage one of induction occurs when a friend decides to tell you of the existence of the club. Vetting has already taken place. Let us assume that you are invited along to the club. This will occur on a special night, in order to avoid disturbing the regulars and to enable a close watch to be kept on you. You will be offered a chance to take what is effectively a series of lessons with help from one or more club members (the use of a 'course' enables the club to invoke 'technical skill' as a reason for later rejection, rather than simply the fact that they 'didn't take to him').

As well as ensuring that the club attracts people who will fit socially, it is also attempting to isolate those who are termed 'cowboys' – people who just want somewhere to mess around, get some practice and then to disappear to take potshots at rabbits on the odd weekend. (We should add that, although the word 'cowboy' has obvious shooting links, its use is widespread in all clubs in relation to those who – like 'pot-hunters' – are just 'using' the group.) On your first night you can make use of the communal equipment but, after a few weeks, you are expected to start thinking of buying your own gun and ancillary equipment. This is a further test of commitment, far more than a 'means test'. After your first few sessions – which will undoubtedly include some time spent at the bar or generally socializing – both you and they will have formed early impressions. You might be told to give up or try another club – you may be too competitive or not competitive enough, too much a receiver and not a contributor, perhaps just too quiet or shy. This changing relationship is not, however, entirely one way; it may be that the group needs time to adapt to you.

In general, however, once the training is over, both you and they will know whether to continue. We have already said that potential new members are warned that they must expect to shoot competitively on a regular basis. This is a further safeguard against both cowboys and loners – those who will merely use the premises rather than participate in a club. However, this particular requirement seems to disappear fairly quickly, though it can always be reintroduced later if an excuse is needed to remove a member. Altogether this process may take upwards of six months and the superficiality of the 'training' can be shown from the fact that no precise performance figure is ever used for acceptance to the club and, once you are a member, it is almost impossible to persuade anybody to give you more training, even if you are performing very badly!

Other clubs use quite formal, advertised classes as a way of attracting new members – photography societies, archery clubs, badminton groups and so on – but even this method often shields more complex social vetting. Two drama group secretaries to whom we spoke said that an ability to act was not a precondition of membership. Neither was an ability to dance for those in the morris men's group. However, performance can be too good. A badminton club identified a potential new member who was 'too keen' and some modelling groups mentioned other members who were 'out of our class'. This seemed more of a problem than the novice, perhaps because it was embarrassing to a greater number, or to the current 'leaders' in the group. Study of such entry and induction processes can show clearly where a group's real concerns lie. In most cases, quite complex vetting procedures lie behind such phrases as 'we are open to anybody, regardless of ability'.

The recruitment and induction procedures are essentially elements of a socialization process through which new members are brought into the culture of the group and the sub-culture of which the group is a part. Of course the socialization process is not a one-way affair. Just as the individual will learn to accommodate to the group, so in time the group will accommodate to its new members. The developing interest of the Charnwood Aquarists' Society in staging its own open show was to no small extent due to the impact of a new member with experience of running shows in his former club. The willingness of a group to accommodate to its members is partly related to the extent to which the group is in demand. This is illustrated in a remark from the treasurer of the West Humberstone Allotment Society in Leicester: 'In years when allotment gardening wasn't so keen, we were only too happy for members to take on as many plots as they wanted. It's only when you've got people on a waiting list that you can bring your standards of gardening up to what you would wish.' In other words, groups that are in demand can afford to be more demanding of their members. We noticed in our research how trampolining, handball and square-dancing groups, for instance, tightened up their recruitment and induction procedures as they moved from a situation where they had too few members to one where they had too many. The reverse does not always apply, however; the Avon Metal Detectors had a membership of over 120 in the early 1970s. When we contacted them in 1982 their membership was down to seven, yet they still carefully vetted all prospective members (fear of 'cowboys' is particularly strong in the organized metal detector sub-culture).

Handling human resources

In Chapter 5 we described a process which we called 'finding a niche'. We sought to show how individuals typically settle into a group by finding a distinctive contribution they can make to it. The other side of this relates to the group's ability to provide opportunities for its members to discover their distinctive competence. Usually the individual member and group quickly discover the right niche within which the individual can flourish. This is particularly the case where one's role in the club is an extension of one's role outside the club. We found that the role of treasurer was often filled by individuals with accounting or administrative backgrounds. It would be wrong, however, to consider that such roles offer no challenge to such individuals – they do provide an extension and not just a replication of a member's existing skills. The following extract from an interview with the secretary of a cricket club in Kingswood (who worked as a manager at the British Aircraft Corporation) makes this clear:

> It's very difficult. Being used to a large firm with a clear structure, straightforward responsibilities, I find that you plan an event, you discuss it with people, you agree what you're going to do and you do it. It's easy when you have people paid to work for you. When they're all volunteers and you discuss the planning of an event, it's the 'feel your way gently' type of approach, which can be very frustrating. When you're dealing with people you're always learning.

There are a number of situations, however, where it is less easy for groups and individual members to discover such a niche. It is almost a truism that any organization cannot make the best use of the skills and resources of its members if it does not have the means by which they can be identified, valued and developed. We have continually stressed the dual nature of communal leisure organizations. The social meaning and value of the group is as important as the substantive focus of its activity. There is a real sense in which the enthusiasm itself is a means through which broader social purposes can be realized. Yet, in virtually every group we studied, a myth was studiously maintained that the social meaning and purpose of the group was subsidiary. As a result it becomes difficult for individual members to talk openly about the social reasons they may have for joining a club or about the contributions they could make which go beyond technical skills or knowledge. It took the social secretary of the Leicester Penguins' Swimming Club five years before she came to her present position. This was not because of competition for this post, but because her own motives, in the context of a strongly competitive club like the Penguins, seemed almost illicit. As she put it:

> You start off by just coming along to watch your lads training and then gradually you start to get involved. You see all these people being very busy and you think they must be important. It's not until you get talking to these people that you realize they're not specialists. You get different types. You get some parents and you're talking to them and all you're talking about is swimming. They can reel their kids' times off from when they were six years old. We were always very interested in the dances. Although I've been very interested in the lads' swimming it is the other side that I've been mosِ interested in.

There can be no doubt that the club now grudgingly realizes that this woman's contribution to the morale and success of its swimmers is second only to the chief coach. The regular round of discos, dances, beetle drives, etc., has attracted many more children to the club than before, and yet this contribution has been made by a member who frankly admitted she found swimming 'a bit boring really'!

This example illustrates the potential loss to a group if it fails to seek out and encourage those skills and resources regarded as secondary to its main purpose. However, it is also essential to add that other losses might accrue if such resources were sought more consciously. Some social objectives for joining a group will probably always seem 'illegitimate' – at least in our society. Despite their clear significance, they remain taboo. It is, however, too easy to view this negatively, to argue that all such motivations and objectives should be clear and open. We suspect that it is often only through operating such motivations at a 'mundane' or 'assumptive' world level that many groups can continue at all. People appear to recognize that they could not deal successfully with all the issues if they were to be made public, and they regard the other bonuses of group membership as outweighing the rather distant potential of more open sharing.

The final issue we would like to raise in this section concerns how a group develops its resources. The observations we make apply particularly to those activities where inter-club competition is fairly intense so that it often gives rise to 'poaching'. This does not occur just in sports like football; we have witnessed the same phenomenon amongst brass bands and drama societies in the Bristol area, amongst bowls clubs in Leicester. Our description of the first year of the Southfields Dynamos illustrates the dilemma facing such clubs. To survive and prosper competitively do you stick with your original core of members or do you start to bring in better players? The danger is that, having become competitive, a group will then abrogate the self-development function that was its original purpose. It is nevertheless quite possible to combine the competitive function with a non-elitist, self-development function. That is, even though the club is engaged in competition, it determines to develop resources rather than trade in them ('poaching' being the most extreme form of trading). In other words, even though the group is now in the Sunday League, it will draw upon the original constituency of the kick-about players from the locality and develop that resource rather than look for quality players 'on the market'. Of course, such a principle can be the excuse for the crudest parochialism and cliquishness; any group whose identity is based on small neighbourhoods or communities runs this risk. On the other hand, the clubs we encountered, such as the Belgrave Casuals Rovers Football Club in Leicester, which deal extensively on the local, informal transfer market, undoubtedly lack the particular sense of identity that Southfields still enjoy.

Coping with change

Coping with change is undoubtedly the most problematic issue for groups, as well as the one which is most likely to bring their 'mundane' or 'assumptive' world to the surface and expose underlying values and aspirations. Change can, however, be viewed in several ways and it will occur for a variety of reasons.

First, one can see change as a natural process. Groups are 'born', pass through a period of 'youth', reach 'middle age' and then – perhaps – 'die'. Some may in fact 'ossify' in later years, or alternatively some may be so responsive to constant change that they become pathologically 'unstable'. Secondly, in counterpoint to this 'natural' cycle, there are several types of changes which can speed or delay natural processes. These can come from within a group – as when members age and their values change over time – or from outside – as, for example, when fashions change or the composition of the local community alters. Finally, one can consider the responses of groups to change. They can ignore it, accommodate to it, or use it positively to influence natural processes such as ageing. We shall deal with each of the above in turn.

Natural processes

It is important to resist the suggestion that these processes are inevitable. Groups are not single organisms and the success of some over fifty years or more shows their often remarkable ability to sustain clear identities and evolve rather than die. The groups of 1985 may be unrecognizable to members from 1935, but the incorporation of new members with new values and the slow exchange of organizational control have all enabled those groups to remain vital, strong and – in some respects – the 'same'.

'Birth' seems to be almost as traumatic for groups as for people, and it has a clear 'mortality' rate. In the early years of a group, almost anything can become a problem – money, premises, affiliating to any association, attracting enough members, deciding on an organization, establishing an identity.

Once past this stage, many groups seem to pass through a period of growth and consolidation which exhibits youthful tendencies of excitement and brashness, extroversion and even evangelism about themselves. The Computers Handball Club (Leicester) remains youthful because its sport is still emerging nationally while Leicester's Overseas Cricket Club retains its youth by constantly seeking new avenues and activities.

Such youthful exuberance more often than not gives way to mature balance. Groups will stop growing, keep members longer, have established premises, develop consistent patterns of organization and exhibit all the signs of a settled group such as social events, local networks, links to associations and so forth. The East Bristol Rifle and Pistol Club and the Conwood Naturalists are at this stage, as were the majority of groups we encountered in Kingswood. It is here, however, that problems may occur. Size can be counter-productive and continued growth can prejudice the qualities sought originally by members. We can offer no magic figure here because different activities require different scales. We merely wish to suggest that the splitting away of one part of a group may often be more appropriate than to try to survive as a totality.

It is also at this stage that ossification can occur, especially when an original core group of members refuses to recognize the inevitability of change and attempts to preserve 'their' group exactly as it was when they set it up. The Conwood Hockey Club clearly illustrated this tension, the 'old guard' both wanting change (for example, newer, younger members, a greater competitiveness) yet also resisting such changes; the two new captains being the unfortunate victims of this ambivalence. The Bitton Light Railway Society in Kingswood also experienced problems of both scale and ossification. Their increasing range of activities necessitated a large, active core of members and the creation of several smaller 'departments' (such as 'Locomotives' or 'Permanent Way'). Each department had, however, become very large in itself and it appeared to us that there was a danger in attempting to stick with a traditional demarcation system (one which is used in British Rail) regardless of its applicability to a non-professional setting.

Obviously, at the time of our research, we encountered no groups which were defunct. We encountered at least one group which was near to death when we contacted the secretary – the Avon Metal Detectors – and we discovered later that they had ceased to exist. When we spoke to members of the Conwood Hockey Club, death seemed far away but the struggle to survive was apparent (and ultimately unsuccessful). Leicester City Council provided us with a long list of groups. We suspect that there were a number with whom contact was impossible because they no longer exist. Death is a natural process, although whether avoidable or not is by no means clear. What became apparent, however, was the view of group death held by many local authority community and leisure services staff. They saw it not as something which is likely to happen to a certain number of groups, but as something to be avoided wherever possible. However, we feel the very idea of holding on to meaningless forms of organizational life should be regarded as naive and sentimental anthropomorphism.

Change from within

Change may arise from a new or growing membership. Members may become old or change residence and leave to be replaced by others with different values and attitudes. A growing group may add more and more people with different attitudes until the original ethos of the group changes. An example of the latter is the Overseas Cricket Club which started with a strong drive solely towards cricket but which has slowly adapted and extended as its membership has grown into something much broader.

Change from within also occurs where groups have a stable and unchanging membership. As these members grow older their attitudes towards competition, 'escape from home' and 'socializing' change as they progress through stages in their life cycle. If a group of members remains constant it is likely that the organization will in fact change quite dramatically, because prevailing values evolve over time. Such change may not, however, be due solely to changes in values; it can also occur if members' material circumstances change. Thus heavy, localized unemployment may dramatically affect the motives of the club members. Paradoxically all the available research suggests that unemployment reduces an individual's motivation towards leisure.[4] Our own research also suggests that the organizational dynamic of communal leisure groups tends to minimize opportunities for the unemployed. For, just as a group tends to have an expectation regarding the minimum level of participation that it sees as legitimate, so it also tends to have expectations regarding maximum levels of permissible participation. Many of our respondents who were unemployed or recently retired were keenly aware that if they put too much time and effort into a group a fragile equilibrium could become upset. The group would become 'lopsided', excessively dependent upon one or two individuals or cajoled into commencing activities for which the majority of members had no desire. As a result, individuals with considerable free time may only be able to consume it by spreading their involvement across a number of activities rather than by concentrating on one.

Change from outside

There are a number of external changes which can affect groups, often in major ways. At a very broad social level there are changes in fashion for certain activities. Handball suffers from being out of fashion, whereas darts, snooker and bowls are experiencing a major surge in popularity. Ice skating and tennis, athletics and horse riding all appear to have minor or major surges related quite closely to the performance of British competitors and there can be little doubt of the connection between television's regular promotion of natural history programmes and the rise in popularity of all forms of wildlife-related activity. The timescale of fashion changes can also be long-term and are not always linear. Cycling was very fashionable in the 1920s and 1930s, went into decline but is now resurfacing strongly. One of the oldest groups we encountered was a cycling club – just celebrating its fiftieth anniversary at the time – and its progress had been very chequered over that period. A further effect of changes in fashion may well be an increasing push towards competitive and professional values within the sub-culture.

Change can occur in groups simply because the local community changes. In Cadbury Heath on the edge of Kingswood, several new estates had introduced a whole range of new people with new values.

It seems likely that the early years of such changes are characterized by new people joining existing groups, then new groups are formed and some of the earlier ones recover something of their original form. We would be surprised if such groups did not exemplify some of the archetypal conflicts and tensions apparent within the changing community itself – in Kingswood we identified two community associations, less than a mile apart and on the same trunk road, one of which had been taken over by 'the newcomers', whereas the other was so dominated by 'the locals' that it had almost no newcomers at all in its membership of over 600.

Response to change

We have already illustrated some of the ways groups cope with change. Groups can ignore change, with the likely outcomes of ossification and death. Groups can choose a period of 'hibernation', generally slowing down, becoming austere, reducing costs and utilizing existing strengths. It was probably such tactics which enabled the cycling club to survive its bleak period in the 1950s and 1960s. A group faced with loss of members can either attempt to legitimate itself elsewhere (as the metal detectors' group tried to do – and failed – in relation to the formal world of archaeology) or expand its definitions or terms of reference. In particular, a small group can adapt its criteria for selecting new members and simply become less exclusive. A group can withdraw selectively from certain external relationships. The Matthews Morris Men manage well with their female musician outside the Morris Ring, but largely because most of their members have roots elsewhere in the morris or folk dancing sub-cultures. The Conwood Naturalists have retreated from the advancing professionalism and evangelism of the conservation movement by refusing to join the county Wildlife Trust. Finally, a group can choose to advance vigorously, like the Overseas Cricket Club or the Soar Valley Gardening Club, both of which seem simply to take on board almost any new initiative which emerges, or any personal aspiration of any member.

The key, however, to the success of groups in coping with inevitable changes is their remarkable ability to retain their identity throughout any change. This is a theme to which we have returned many times. In the face of myriad pressures from individuals, from the environment and from internal structures, it seems almost miraculous that a range of clear and easily identifiable groups emerges.

On many occasions during our research, when commenting on their own group, respondents found it easier to offer a description through a comparison of their group with others in the area or within their activity. These 'photofit' sketches served to place their own group and all others in a series – some were too competitive, others too 'cliquey', a few were too big, some just not 'professional' enough. The fact that others from the same group would offer slightly different sketches, or that members of the other groups might well reverse the same points ('they're the ones who are too competitive'), does little to destroy the general sense of clear and relatively stable identities within each group.

We gained the distinct impression that a successful group is one in which it is possible for the identity of that group to remain coherent even after its original membership has left – in other words, there is an identity which is far more than merely the sum of its members at one particular moment. While we have acknowledged that there are a number of existing and potential tensions lying behind the façades of many groups, their assertive independence was a very striking feature for us as outsiders. We feel sure that the vast majority of group members have an unconscious realization of the value – the preciousness – of what they are involved with and we hope we have demonstrated its existence and strength to the reader. Our task in the final chapter will be to offer some more general conclusions on the implications of what we have been studying for wider social concerns and to briefly look at current changes in that wider society which could prove very difficult for groups to handle and which could, if developed in ignorance, damage this valuable territory beyond repair.

Chapter 8

Conclusions

As our research developed, it seemed as though we had stumbled into an area of social life which was massive in its proportions, rich in detail and of fascinating complexity, but almost completely overlooked. The two of us have had extensive involvement in various other forms of community action, both in a 'voluntary' and salaried capacity, yet we were surprised by the nature and scale of the groups that we encountered. Moreover, we have found that our ignorance is shared not just by virtually all the 'professional' community activists to whom we have spoken, but also by recreational planners, local councillors, other local and central government officers and even by many community workers operating from various forms of local action centres. This collective blind spot by policy makers and implementors is of central importance.

Why should we talk of discovery, when, after all, some of the clubs we encountered had been in existence for decades? We can only suggest that the 'invisibility' of this aspect of social life is in large part due to traditionally narrow concepts of 'leisure' and 'voluntarism'.

Let us examine the concept of leisure and specifically the manner in which it has been construed by those broadly situated on the political 'left' in our society. Over the last couple of years we have often found ourselves arguing with community activists (who are rarely themselves 'of' the community but who have 'parachuted' into one) who have said that all this emphasis on leisure is very well but it is not the real stuff of local action. One often gained the impression that amateur cricketers, caged bird enthusiasts and so on were considered an interesting but exasperating novelty (if only they would devote their organizing energies to really important community issues such as tenants' associations or the fight against cuts). In other words, leisure is construed as a kind of diversionary and placatory activity, even in its more active and self-organized forms. A similar but perhaps even more uncompromising attitude is held by many academic and political writers who are even less 'close to the ground', for they talk about leisure as if it were the modern opium of the masses – a form of mindless escapism or orchestrated passivity. Many Marxists, for example, see leisure purely in terms of another sphere of social control, a form of mass consumption in which we are all titillated, duped and satiated by advanced capitalism's 'captains of

consciousness' (marketeers, advertisers, journalists, leisure techno-
crats, etc.). A distinct strand of recent academic Marxist writing[1]
therefore sees leisure merely as one more site of domination, as
something which contributes to the atomization and privatization of
society, reinforces the withdrawal of the working class from public
life and further undermines its capacity for self-organization.

If leisure were to be construed solely as an element of
consumption, then we would readily agree that the prospect of it
acquiring an emancipatory potential would be slim indeed. At first
sight this is how it seems, for surely we are producers when at work
and consumers when at home?

However, if we consider the individual as a producer only when
engaged in the imaginative transformation of the given into
something new (a process Marx refers to as 'objectification'), then it is
clear that the vast majority of individuals no longer exist as producers
when at work, rather they exist as a 'factor of production' which is
consumed and worn out along with the other factors of the
productive process (machines, buildings). At the heart of the modern
factory and office system lies a very special form of the division of
labour, the separation of imagination from execution, of head from
hands, of thinking from doing. As a result the worker engages in the
process of transforming raw material in accordance with another's
imagination. The worker realizes another's idea, and is subject to, but
no longer the subject of, the labour process.

Standing appearance on its head, we can now see how the vast
majority of workers are not producers when at work, rather they are
consumed by work and therefore can only confirm themselves as
imaginative, self-determining beings outside of work. Hence the
importance of understanding leisure in its productive and self-
organized forms. One of the few writers on the left to have
acknowledged the crucial importance of this sphere of human activity
is André Gorz. Gorz has consistently drawn attention to what he calls
the sphere of 'autonomous production' lying outside the formal
private and public sector economies. As he notes:

> The sphere of individual sovereignty is not based on a mere
> desire to consume... it is based more profoundly on activities
> .... which are in themselves communication, giving, creating
> and aesthetic enjoyment, the production and reproduction of
> life, tenderness, the realisation of physical, sensuous and
> intellectual capacities, the creation of non-commodity use-
> values (shared goods or services).[2]

We feel that the term 'leisure' has become so strongly associated
with consumerism that it may be difficult to 'reclaim' it in the way we
would like. Perhaps the term 'leisure' is therefore best left to refer

merely to forms of consumerism. But if such activity is not leisure, what is it? We feel there is a strong argument to be made for considering the productive activities of our enthusiasts as an everyday form of cultural production. It is time to break away from seeing a nation's culture solely in terms of its finest paintings or dramas. We must develop a non-elitist notion in which it is seen to be located in its everyday forms – its back gardens, kitchens, playing fields, sheds-cum-workshops, hobbies, and so on. Virtually each one of us, every day, is involved in some form of cultural production. It may be as simple as writing a letter or cultivating a pond in the back garden. The point is that we do it for pleasure rather than out of necessity or obligation and, moreover, the activity involves us as 'tool-using animals' in a process of confronting the given with our subjectivity, our imagination, patience, love and aggression. Out of this something is created which had never existed before. Over a thousand games of football may be played on a single playing field, yet each one will be different; a thousand children can sit before the same flower yet each would paint something new. As, in our enthusiasm, we work, we consume both our means of production (pen, paper, ink, etc.) and our own living powers. Such activity is freely given ('voluntary', if you like) but then all leisure is by definition voluntary rather than coerced or of necessity.

The concepts of 'voluntarism' and 'voluntary sector' are not only inappropriate when applied to this area; they are in fact quite dangerous. The idea of asking a member of an angling club or drama society how long she had been involved in this voluntary activity is bizarre, but no more bizarre than insisting that lapidary societies, archery clubs and military modelling associations are all part of a 'voluntary sector in leisure'. But the idea that such a sector exists is fast becoming a firm article of belief within both central and local government, particularly within the newly emergent leisure profession. Professionalization corresponds to the monopolization of certain areas of human life by particular occupational groups who establish rights over 'their territory' by gaining state legitimation for their claim to have the singular knowledge, experience and skill to tackle that area of social need.[3] 'Leisure' therefore must become a social problem before professionalization can occur, and one can be sure that the aspirant 'leisure profession' will do all in its power to ensure that leisure does become construed in just this functionalist way. Thus the emergent profession is already speaking in terms of 'leisure lack'[4] as if it were an identifiable syndrome requiring attention in the same way as a vitamin deficiency, or whatever. Similarly there emerges the concept of 'leisure counselling', 'leisure careers' (as people pass through stages of the life cycle they develop new leisure interests and therefore can be seen as having a distinct leisure career), and so on. A whole new language emerges, a professional jargon that bestows an apparent legitimacy and rationality upon what is in fact a process of domination.

The idea of the existence of a 'voluntary sector in leisure' is therefore an essential element in the world view of the leisure profession and the state formations which it snuggles inside. Indeed the state, whether at central or local level, needs a 'voluntary sector' to deal with and relate to, because, despite being a fiction, the concept suggests the existence of something which is apparently coherent and simple and therefore easy to manage. We should perhaps speak of a process of 'sectorization' out of which a 'sector' is eventually produced. Something like this almost undoubtedly developed in the sphere of health and social care many decades ago. There can be little doubt that in the late nineteenth century most social care was self-organized, either informally through the family or more formally through the same kinds of mutual aid organizations that dominate the sphere of leisure today. The professionalization of health and social care has been built upon the removal of the functions and competences of families and communities.[5] The self-organization of such activity then becomes a residual phenomenon sapped of vitality and reluctantly amenable to being constituted as a 'voluntary sector', whose role is largely to fill the gaps in state provision. It is precisely the prospect of the same thing happening in leisure that fills us with such foreboding. If we were to sum up our impressions of the current attitudes of the emergent leisure professionals, we would describe them as leisure 'evangelism', with all the both negative and positive connotations of that word. This is not to say that the state (and its professions) has no role to play.[6] Rather it is to argue that this role should be to nurture, encourage and enable rather than to disable, monopolize and control (as in the worst of evangelism). Moreover, our argument is not just with the professionalized state but with the socialist and social democratic political parties who, in Britain, have for decades confused 'collectivism' with 'statism', whether in the spheres of public ownership or public service. There is still an incredibly strong 'statism' discernible throughout the whole spectrum of the British left which may well have something to do with the fact that most leftists spend their leisure engaged in the politics of either managing the state or planning its take-over, unlike the majority of most normal people whose leisure leads them into a world of organization quite outside the state.

We hope we have made it clear that this so-called voluntary sector in leisure is in fact comprized of a myriad of fragments. Far from there being the commonality and coherence of a sector, we find a series of vertical sub-cultures. These sub-cultures are so distinct and complex that it is difficult enough to persuade an athlete, tennis player and gymnast on a local sports council that they have anything much in common, let alone bring together sports, arts, crafts, hobbies and pastimes into a voluntary leisure sector!

But let us assume for a moment that the public and private sectors had taken over the organization of the bulk of productive leisure activities. What would it cost Leicester City Council just to organize amateur football in the area? Let us assume that the chairman, secretary, treasurer and manager of each club together put in about eight hours' work a week (though this is undoubtedly a gross underestimate). There are well over 200 adult and youth teams playing within the city so, on the basis of our calculations, the city council would need to hire about forty 'community leisure officers' just to sustain football in the area. And then what about the referees, the people who organize the local leagues, and so on? We are talking about a £1 million operation just to organize this one activity, but then the clubs also provide their own kit, balls, goal posts and, in a few instances, their own pavilions and pitches as well! If we were to attach a market value to all the activities of local enthusiasts, it would easily dwarf the £15 million per annum that Leicester currently spends on leisure. But all of this economic activity goes uncounted. It does not contribute to estimates of our gross national product. It is a part of the hidden economy of our society.

It would be useful at this point to try out yet another way of looking at the organization of enthusiasms. Jonathan Gershuny[7] has proposed that we might look at the economy as a whole as comprising a number of distinct sectors. The primary sector includes the 'extractive' industries, such as mining, agriculture, etc. The secondary sector comprises the manufacturing industries. The tertiary sector is the service economy, both private and public. And the informal sector comprises household and domestic work, communal activity and the black economy.

Leagues, etc., that have been our focus are an element of what Gershuny would call 'the informal communal economy'. It is important to remind ourselves that the term 'communal' should not be used to refer only to organizations within a particular local community. As we have illustrated, many 'local' clubs may be organized on a district basis which covers several 'localities', particularly if, as with lapidarism, the activity is fairly esoteric or if the club only caters for enthusiasts with high levels of demonstrated competence.

Leisure sub-cultures clearly straddle both formal and informal sectors of the economy. Quite recently the state attempted to claw back benefits from a number of unemployed anglers in Shropshire. It was argued that the trout that they caught for their own consumption and for barter and sale with friends and neighbours affected their entitlement to state aid. The activity of such anglers can be seen as an illustration of what Gershuny means by the informal domestic and black economies. If they are also members of a club which owns or leases its own stretch of water, then their activity as club members corresponds to that appropriate to the informal communal economy. We are using angling simply to illustrate that many leisure sub-cultures have their roots within all three elements of the informal economy. We found this particularly to be the case for most arts, crafts and hobbies. The homes of the enthusiasts we interviewed were typically crammed with their own products – tapestries, framed pictures and photographs, wines, honey, gem stones, models and so on. We found that very often they were also engaged in the black economy; rarely on a scale sufficient to provide them with a living wage, but enough to provide them with a bit of pin money which would almost invariably be ploughed back into their enthusiasm. We feel the phrase 'pocket money work'[8] usefully describes the scale and function of this very widespread element of the black economy.[9] Such pocket money helps provide enthusiasts with their means of production, for example, angling equipment, canvas, lapidary machinery and so on. The leisure sub-culture is therefore a phenomenon that involves both the informal and the secondary (manufacturing) sectors of the economy, but not the tertiary sector. As we argued previously it is only when the professionalized state begins to penetrate and take over what was previously organized within the informal sector that such sub-cultural formations become transformed into 'public service'. It is equivalent to a shift in economic activity from the informal to the tertiary sector of the economy.

Our own values lead us to view the possibility of such a shift with alarm. We feel that the activities of such sub-cultures and of the clubs, federations and individuals which they comprize are a vital but overlooked element of our culture. The celebration of such forms of self-organization is a necessary part of the struggle for the development of convivial social relationships in the face of urban anonymity and the omnipresent state.[10]

The natural but thwarted sociability of humankind is something we all too easily take for granted. The very question 'Why do people join groups?' is one designed to mislead us. Just as Wilhelm Reich once said, 'The question is not why do some people steal but why do poor people not steal?', so our own question should properly be rephrased as 'Why do some people not join groups?' The substantive purpose of a football club or drama society, whilst important, is no more important than the social purpose of such organizations and the sub-cultures of which they are a part. Such forms of organization constitute a place 'to do', but also, and crucially, a place 'to be'. An understanding that much self-organization is an 'end in itself' besides being a 'means to an end' (something grasped by anarchists such as Kropotkin almost a hundred years ago[11]), seems to have been lost by many community activists today. It would be tempting but misplaced to try to apply some of the principles of community development and organizational development to communal leisure organizations. Certainly, many of those groups are indeed parochial and un-dynamic; many more are quite content steadily to tick over – they may have ambitions but these are measured very carefully. That is why many of these groups have been around for fifty years or more (far longer than the welfare state itself). The danger is that in attempting to develop a community's sense of its strength and resourcefulness, development workers will consider only the one side of a group's existence; community organizations will be improved in their 'doing' at the expense of their 'being' – a typically male orientation.

Finally, we wish to consider mutual aid. We have argued consistently that most communal leisure groups can be considered as organized forms of mutual aid – in this case, as vehicles through which people can help each other to pleasure. Strangely enough, one often encounters a viewpoint which suggests that such organizations, because of their self-interest, cannot also serve the community. The following extract from a memorandum circulating within a large state-controlled, grant-giving body illustrates our point. The mem-orandum outlines the various criteria to be used in judging when a community organization is suitable for grant aid: a key criterion refers to 'bodies which exist to service a membership without a direct public commitment but which may undertake projects or events of wider public interest'. In other words, mutual aid organizations are held to have no 'direct public commitment' and will only be eligible for grant aiding if some of their activities are of 'wider public interest'. But why on earth should it be thought that if the public combine together to service themselves, their activity somehow or another fails to express direct public commitment? Do we have two 'publics', a real one which does nothing and therefore needs servicing and a not quite legitimate one which presumes to organize in its own exclusive self-interest? How is the community 'best served'? By being helped to help itself as self-interest transforms itself without difficulty into a commitment to mutuality, or by being helped to remain helpless? The point we are trying to make may seem paradoxical: that mutual aid is founded upon self-interest or, more accurately, upon an identity of self-interest.

As Kropotkin and others have argued, self-interest is in fact the firmest foundation for cultural and political organization. The 'sectionalism' of many kinds of organization – trade unions, tenants' associations or amateur sports clubs – is in fact far more often a problem for public sector managers and political activists than for those organizations themselves. Sectionalism is a crucial element of the strength of such organizations, both as an expression of the immediacy and concreteness of whatever theme brings members together and as a form of defence against homogenizing external pressures such as 'sectorization'. How one facilitates movement from the particular to the general, from narrow and parochial concerns to broader cultural perspectives has been a dilemma for the socialist movement since its very foundations. One part of the answer is clear, however – the trick is not to be achieved by berating such organizations for their sectionalism. Inasmuch as the identity of any group we have studied is both totally dependent upon and yet also more than the sum of its parts, so any construct such as broader culture cannot exist without its many sections or parts. One cannot learn to ride a horse by tying its legs together!

There is, however, a key difference between communal leisure organizations and others such as trade unions or tenants' associations. The self-interest of the latter is based upon overt need, whereas in communal leisure we are speaking of that realm of human life beyond such need. Whereas need always carries with it the force of necessity: 'Beyond it begins that development of human energy which is an end in itself, the true realm of freedom which however can blossom forth only with this realm of necessity as its base.'[12]

Leisure, then, begins beyond need. The self-interest underlying forms of communal leisure is therefore not based upon neediness, but upon enthusiasm, pleasure and enjoyment. It may perhaps be more useful to talk about an enthusiast's desires than needs. For many activities it is then only through coming together that one can fulfil certain desires, those not available to the individual acting alone.

However, we should be very wary of a purely instrumental concept of organizing. The clubs and associations described in this book are not merely settings in which people 'do' things; they were no mere means to ends. The organizations themselves are creations of groups of enthusiasts and no less 'works of art' than the external products which flow from them. The groups are places to 'be' as much as to 'do', with their own histories, characters, dramas and meanings. Our culture is so 'white', male and pragmatic that we often lose sight of the fact that life is not only about 'doing things'. Any erosion of places to 'be' must surely be regarded as retrograde. Yet current trends might well lead to such erosion.

We have already mentioned changes in the leisure professions and the growth of leisure 'evangelism'. Part of this includes an approach rooted in instrumental and functionalist thinking about leisure and which we call the 'development ethic'. We are anxious that this philosophy will encourage efforts to 'improve', 'raise the standard of', 'widen interest in' and generally 'develop' what groups 'do' at the expense of what they 'are'. This in turn relates to growing tendencies to apply to the 'voluntary sector' notions of organizational management and development adapted from the progressive end of the private sector.

The theory and practice of management has been based upon organizations which are primarily in the business of producing things. There can be no doubt that factories, social services departments, etc., provide their members with 'a place to be' as well as with tasks to perform, but nevertheless their overwhelming concern is with the latter, that is with outputs. Thus, when one speaks of 'organizational development', it is always with a view to the quality and quantity of organizational output. Communal leisure organizations are, to our mind, quite different. Their wider social purposes cannot be subordinated to the tasks and objectives they set themselves. In fact they 'walk on both legs': they 'do things', but at their leisure. They are productive without being burdened by the productive imperative of the formal economy. It would be a profound mistake to look at the superficially cumbersome committee of the Redland Ladies' Hockey Club through the eyes of the productive mode of the formal economy and then attempt to apply to such organizations alien philosophies such as 'efficiency and effectiveness'.

In this conclusion we have focused primarily on dangers from state 'colonialism'. There is, however, another set of pressures which we have addressed only incidentally in this book – that inherent in the commercialization and commodification of communal leisure. We have looked at the current impingement by the commercial world on communal leisure and how strong sub-cultural formations can negotiate, adapt or even subvert such pressures. In this context we consider that the search for pure, oppositional, working-class sub-cultures is as misplaced as the attempt to demonstrate the total dominance of a one-dimensional 'commodity' form over all realms of life. Rather we see a series of sub-cultural formations infused with contradictory values and, while we have offered some anecdotal insights into how such contradictions are resolved, we would be the first to admit that this is an area for further work. Finally, it is worth mentioning here that other very broad pressures can also be exerted upon leisure sub-cultures. In a recent study of the Scottish sport of shinty, Whitson[13] argues that increased regionalism, improved transport, pressures for a single Scottish cultural tradition, changing employment markets and so on are all leading to a decline in the status of and involvement in the sport. But, as we have said before, we cannot resort to sentimental romanticism and consider all such changes to be inevitably destructive.

So all around us change is taking place and yet, while clearly not wishing to preserve 'redundant species', we are concerned that in ten or twenty years' time what we have described in this book will have become history; mere illustrations of how we used to live. We hope we have conveyed to the reader some of our sense of enjoyment at what we were privileged to experience and that we also succeeded in drawing attention to the precious and threatened nature of the territory. Diverse and complex, some help and support is clearly needed, if only to rectify the imbalances in distribution at which we have hinted. It may well be, however, that the best we can do is to understand and appreciate better... then leave alone.

References

Chapter 1: Introduction
1. For example, I. Sealey, *Outdoor Recreation and the Urban Environment*, London: Macmillan, 1973.
2. *Report of the Joint Working Party on Recreation Research*, SSRC/Sports Council, (unpublished).
3. For example, *The Rationale for Public Sector Involvement in Leisure*; a project being undertaken at the Centre for Leisure Research, Dunfermline College, Edinburgh. (Reports due 1985/6, contact Roger Sidaway.)
4. A. Tomlinson, *Leisure and the Role of Clubs and Voluntary Groups*, London, SSRC/Sports Council, 1979.
5. P. Hoggett and J. Bishop, *The Social Organisation of Leisure: A Study of Groups in Their Voluntary Sectror Context*, London, SSRC/Sports Council, 1985.

Chapter 3: Mutual aid in leisure
1. For a more detailed analysis of race and sport in Leicester, see Hoggett and Bishop.
2. John, Baron Wolfenden, *The Future of Voluntary Organisation*, Report of the Wolfenden Committee, London: Croom Helm, 1978.
3. For two contrasting views, see F. Mount, 'Liberation Beyond Socialism's Garden Gate', *Guardian*, 28 June 1985, and a reply by G. Jones, 'Taking Stock of Productive Resources', 5 July 1985.

Chapter 4: Leisure sub-cultures
1. Johnson, R., 'Three Problematics: Elements of a Theory of Working Class Cultures', in J. Clarke, C. Crichter and R. Johnson (Eds.), *Working Class Culture*, London: Hutchinson, 1979, p. 233-4.
2. Becker, H. S., 'Art as Collective Action', *American Sociological Review*, 1974, Vol. 39, p. 772.
3. Gorz, A., *Farewell to the Working Class*, London: Pluto Press, 1983.
4. See also Crichter, C., 'Football Since the War', in Clarke, Crichter and Johnson.

Chapter 5. The contribution of individuals to groups
1. See K. Young and E. Mills, *Understanding the Assumptive World of Governmental Actors*, Report to the SSRC Panel on Central/Local Relations, London, 1978, and R. H. Brown, 'Bureaucracy as Praxis: Toward a Political Phenomenology of Formal Organisations', *Administrative Science Quarterly*, 1978, Vol. 23, pp. 365-82.
2. J. Piaget, *The Development of Thought: Equilibration of Cognitive Structures*, Oxford: Blackwell, 1978.
3. Piaget.
4. J. Brandenburg *et al.*, 'A Conceptual Model of How People Adopt Leisure Activities', *Leisure Studies*, 1, 1982, p. 263-76.

Chapter 6: The environment of groups
1. K. Koffka, *Principles of Gestalt Psychology*, London: Kegan Paul, 1935.
2. H. Gans, *The Levittowners*, New York: Vintage; 1967.
3. See S. McConnell, *Theories for Planning*, London: Heinemann, 1981.
4. M. Webber, 'The Urban Place and the Non-Place Urban Realm', in *Explorations into Urban Structure*, Philadelphia: University of Pennsylvania Press, 1963.
5. For four divergent views, see M. Castells, 'Crisis, Planning and the Quality of Life', in *Environment and Planning*, 1983, Vol. 1, pp. 3-22. R. Hall, D. Thorns and

W. Willmott, 'Community, Class and Kinship', in *Environment and Planning*, 1984, Vol. 2, pp. 201–15. J. Porrit, *Seeing Green*, Oxford: Blackwell, 1985. J. Seabrook, *The Idea of Neighbourhood*, London: Pluto Press, 1984.
6. A Twelvetrees, *Community Associations and Centres: A Comparative Study*, Oxford: Pergamon, 1976. A. Tomlinson, 'The Illusion of Community: Cultural Values and Meaning of Leisure in a Gentrifying Neighbourhood', in A. Tomlinson (Ed.), *Leisure and Popular Cultural Forms*, Brighton: Brighton Polytechnic, 1983.

Chapter 7: The structure and dynamic of communal leisure organisations
1. F. Bailey (Ed.), *Gifts and Poisons: The Politics of Reputation*, Oxford: Blackwell, 1971.
2. J. Gershuny, 'The Informal Economy', in *Futures*, 1979, Vol. 11, p. 6.
3. Young and Mills.
4. I. Miles, *Adaptation to Unemployment*, SPRU Occasional Paper No. 20, Falmer: Sussex University, 1983.

Chapter 8: Conclusions
1. H. Marcuse, *One Dimensional Man*, London: Routledge and Kegan Paul, 1964.
2. Gorz.
3. P. Wilding, *Professional Power and Social Welfare*, London: Routledge and Kegan Paul, 1982.
4. J. Neulinger, 'Leisure Lack and the Quality of Life', *Leisure Studies*, 1983, Vol. 2, No. 3.
5. I. Illich *et al*, *Disabling Professions*, London: Marion Boyars, 1977.
6. Hoggett and Bishop, pp. 79–90.
7. Gershuny.
8. Charles Handy, *The Informal Economy*, ARVAC Pamphlet No. 3, 1982.
9. Unfortunately by construing the informal economy solely in terms of the category 'informal work', Pahl's important research on the Isle of Sheppey concludes that there is little evidence of an informal communal economy on the island. We are sure that a great deal of self-organized leisure does occur on the island but it is unlikely that locals construe this in terms of informal 'work'. R. Pahl, *Divisions of labour*, Oxford: Blackwell, 1984.
10. E. Cherki and D. Mehl, *Les Voies de la Contestation Urbane*, Venice: University of Venice, unpublished paper, 1978.
11. P. Kropotokin, *Mutual Aid*, New York: Porter Sargent, 1904, reprinted 1976.
12. K. Marx, *Capital*, Vol. 1, London: Lawrence and Wishart, 1970, pp. 805–6.
13. D. Whitson, 'Pressures on Regional Games in a Dominant Metropolitan Culture', *Leisure Studies*, 1983, Vol. 2, pp. 139–54.

Organizations and Democracy Series

No. 1   **WHAT A WAY TO RUN A RAILROAD — an analysis of
        radical failure** by Charles Landry, David Morley, Russell
        Southwood and Patrick Wright
        £2.50 paperback only

No. 2   **ORGANIZING AROUND ENTHUSIASMS: Patterns of
        Mutual Aid in Leisure** by Jeff Bishop and Paul Hoggett
        £5.95 paperback only

No. 3   **BAD SOLUTIONS TO GOOD PROBLEMS: The
        Practice of Organizational Change** by Liam Walsh
        £3.95, paperback only, Spring 1986